Country Dollmaking

by Nancy and Tom Wolfe

Schiffer Publishing Ltd

1469 Morstein Road, West Chester, Pennsylvania 19380

DEDICATION

This book is dedicated to our parents, James and Eva Brackman, and Bill and Melzina Wolfe.

Printed in the United States of America.
ISBN: 0-88740-129-5
Published by Schiffer Publishing Ltd.
1469 Morstein Road, West Chester, Pennsylvania 19380

This book may be purchased from the publisher.
Please include $2.00 postage.
Try your bookstore first.

Contents

ACKNOWLEDGMENTS

Thanks go to Dorothy Friedhoff and Gwen Wells, long-time dollmakers and old friends whose advice and support made the dolls a reality.

Introduction

In almost every culture and every time people have cherished their dolls. Most of the time they were, like today, toys, and they helped children to learn something about life through fantasy and play. But sometimes they were more serious things, objects of worship, totems, symbols, and in our modern culture valued and valuable collectibles. From the ancient Egyptians who buried dolls with their departed loved ones to the Barbies of today, much can be told about a culture by its dolls.

Long before giant toy stores had row after row of every imaginable type of doll for children to choose, people used to make their own. Using whatever materials were available, they fashioned small creatures that delighted the children. In the South during and after the Civil War, when materials were scarce, parents fashioned handkerchief dolls for their children. In rural America many beautiful dolls have been made from corn husks. In West Virginia dolls were carved from coal. Paper mache was always a popular material and so was wood. Wood was used by the Egyptians. American Indians carved wonderful wooden dolls. In the great farm country of Pennsylvania, when peddlers had to travel long distances between farmsteads, they would carve a wooden doll between stops, knowing that they would have a waiting customer.

So the Wolfes are part of a great tradition and are sharing that tradition with you the reader. Tom Wolfe, coming from a family of carvers, started carving at a young age and because he likes carving faces, dolls came naturally to him. The first doll he carved was used to illustrate a book called *The First Hundred Years of Hittie*, the story of a doll and its adventures. Later Tom took a movable wooden figure he made, Dancin' Sam, enlarged the features and made them more elaborate until it became a doll.

Nancy also started young with her sewing, and in about the seventh grade things started looking the way she meant them to. She took formal sewing classes in Junior and Senior High School and was always encouraged at home. Her father got sewing kits for her at Christmas and they were a favorite present. In fact, she still has some placemats from the first embroidery kit he gave her.

Nancy even learned a sewing lesson from her father. Her mother's sewing machine was next to Nancy's parent's bed. She let Nancy use it for a project. Since it was so convenient, Nancy used the bed for a pincushion. That night her father discovered her cleverness in a most painful way, and taught Nancy a lesson she has never forgotten: Never use a bed for a pincushion.

Despite this small set-back, Nancy continued her career in sewing. She's made stuffed toys and Barbie clothes, and has worked in a couple of sewing factories. She also sews clothes for Tom to wear at shows and exhibitions. Although she enjoys sewing she does not find it particularly relaxing. She is always working hard to make her craft better.

Nancy and Tom's talents were brought together by two friends, Dorothy Friedhof and Gwen Wells who are doll enthusiasts. They had been trying to get Tom to carve dolls for a long time. He thought it was a good idea but could never really find the time, until one year when they were all together at Rockingham Junior High School for a folk arts seminar with the students. The four of them, Tom, Nancy, Dorothy and Gwen combined their talents to create a doll. Tom carved, Gwen painted, Dorothy made the body and hair, and Nancy made the clothes. The result was a Grandma doll that is now in the Antique Museum at Mystery Hill.

Tom and Nancy continued making dolls after that and found a great demand for them in their shop, also at Mystery Hill, in Blowing Rock, North Carolina. Some were all wood, many were Dolly Parton look-alikes (Tom says), and some were made with cloth bodies. But gradually they began to produce primarily young, not terribly attractive children, like the one in this book.

"Why are your dolls so ugly?" a woman asked Tom at a show once. Tom looked around and said, "I figured God must really love ugly people....., 'cause he made so many of them."

The truth is Tom never carves a "pretty" doll. They are not cutsy because Tom strives to make them look like people. Usually when he is carving he is thinking of someone he knows, an aunt, a friend, a neighbor. While the doll may not look at all like that person, there is something of that person's spirit in it, even if only for Tom.

Tom likes to say the dolls look like Cinderella's step sisters, but Nancy doesn't agree. "Cinderella's step sisters were mean," she argues, "but these dolls are anything but mean."

Once at a juried show a judge approached Tom's dolls from the back. She later told Tom that she said to herself, "Oh no! Not another cutsy doll." But when she saw the front of the doll she saw an imp that "looked like she would steal your ice cream."

The clothing for the doll is complete, including the bloomers, Nancy is quick to point out. Someone once told her she didn't need them, with the cloth body and the full dress. "Oh yes you do," said Nancy. "You watch a woman looking at a doll and the very first thing she'll do is pull up the dress to see if it has underwear. While the slip is not always mandatory, no proper doll will go out without her bloomers."

From their "realistic" faces to their bloomers these dolls are delightful. And they are fun to make. This is Tom's third carving book and he and Nancy both are able to lead even the beginner easily through the steps of making these dolls. We hope you enjoy them and that the doll you make will become a treasured possession for you.

Douglas Congdon-Martin, Editor
Schiffer Publishing Ltd.

The Carving

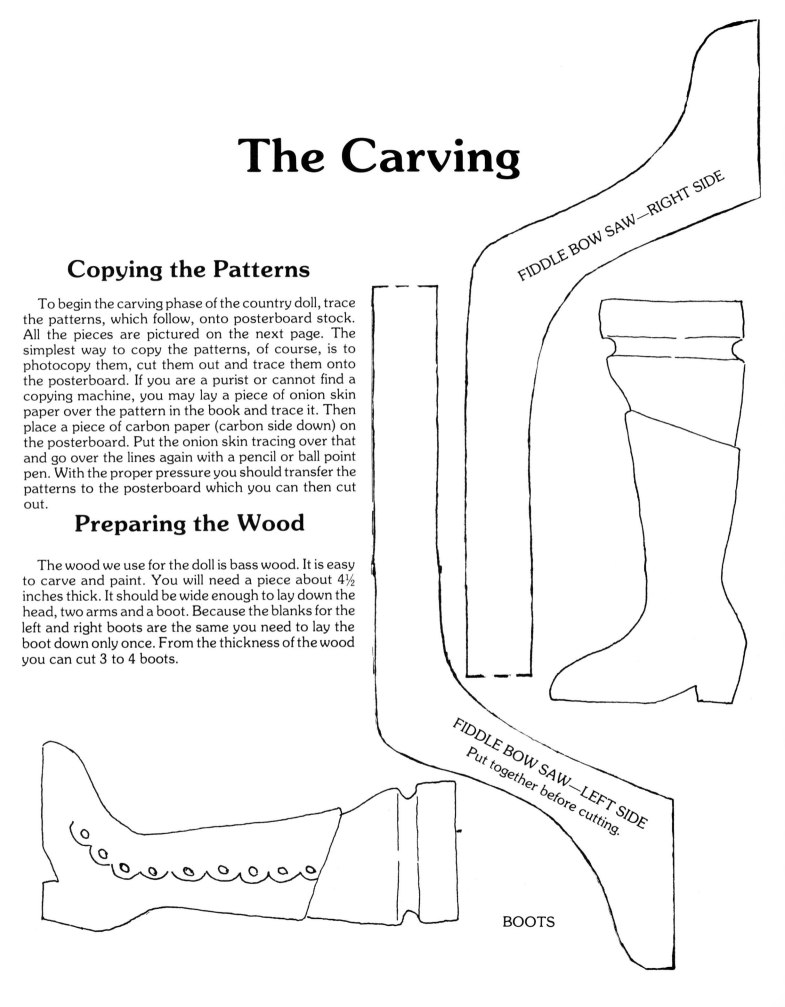

Copying the Patterns

To begin the carving phase of the country doll, trace the patterns, which follow, onto posterboard stock. All the pieces are pictured on the next page. The simplest way to copy the patterns, of course, is to photocopy them, cut them out and trace them onto the posterboard. If you are a purist or cannot find a copying machine, you may lay a piece of onion skin paper over the pattern in the book and trace it. Then place a piece of carbon paper (carbon side down) on the posterboard. Put the onion skin tracing over that and go over the lines again with a pencil or ball point pen. With the proper pressure you should transfer the patterns to the posterboard which you can then cut out.

Preparing the Wood

The wood we use for the doll is bass wood. It is easy to carve and paint. You will need a piece about 4½ inches thick. It should be wide enough to lay down the head, two arms and a boot. Because the blanks for the left and right boots are the same you need to lay the boot down only once. From the thickness of the wood you can cut 3 to 4 boots.

FIDDLE BOW SAW—RIGHT SIDE

FIDDLE BOW SAW—LEFT SIDE
Put together before cutting.

BOOTS

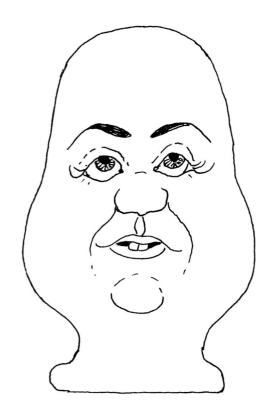
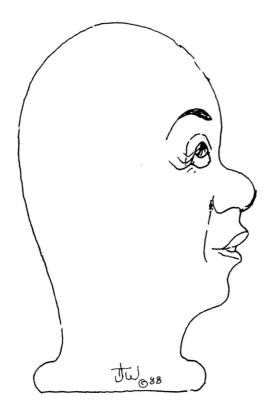

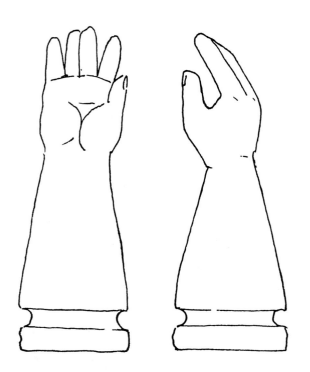
ARMS
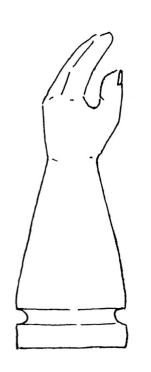
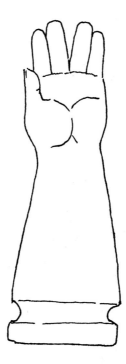

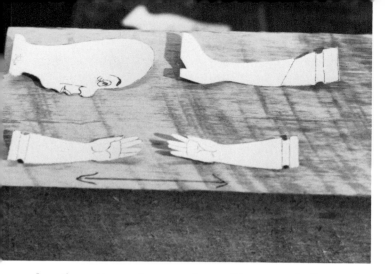

Lay the patterns down as shown. The arrow indicates the direction of the grain.

Cut the board in half above the boot for easier working.

Trace the patterns onto the wood.

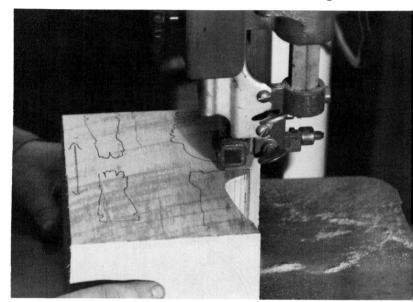

Then cut out the shape.

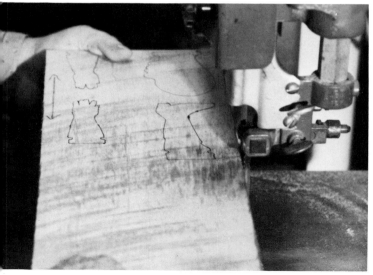

Begin by bandsawing the boot. When using the bandsaw keep the heels of your hands on the table and push with your fingers.

When the shape is out, cut the boot in half. The boot will be 1¼ inches wide.

Since cracks in the wood are likelier near the surface, measure the 1¼ inches from this middle cut, and cut again.

When finished cutting the rough shape of a piece, check for any problems in the wood. In this case there is a bad section that we want to avoid.

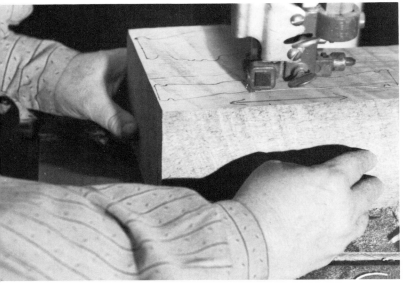

Begin cutting the arms by cutting straight down the side.

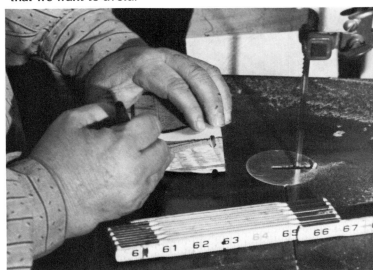

The arms will be about as thick as they are wide, in this case about 1¼ inches. Mark off the space you will use and lay the profile of the arm on the blank and mark.

Finish cutting the arm patterns.

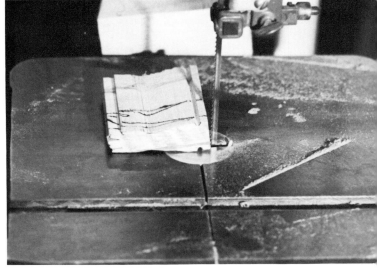

Bandsaw along the profile.

Do the same with the other arm, making certain that you have a left and right arm by laying the blanks side-by-side.

then come back and carefully cut in the details of the face.

Before starting the head, mark and cut small lines straight to the top of the head and to the bottom of the neck.

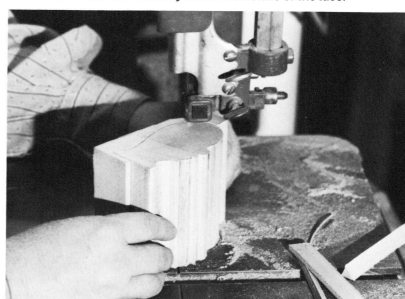

When the face is finished you will carefully cut around the back of the head. You want this to be a single cut...

Roughly cut around the front of the head...

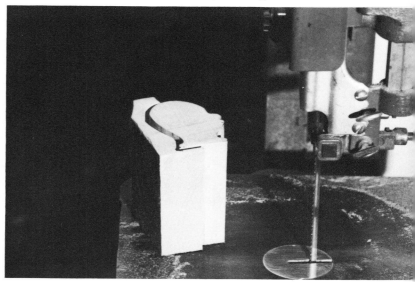

so the excess wood will serve as a cradle for further work on the head.

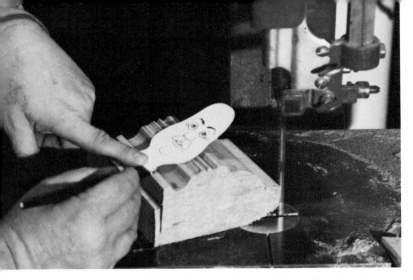 

Place the head back down in the cradle and lay the face-on pattern on it. Starting with the bottom edge, mark the pattern on the blank.

Work your way up the pattern a section at a time until it is complete. Don't try to bend the pattern to do it all at once, as this would distort the face.

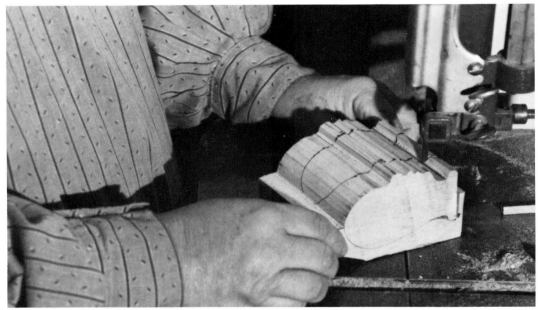

When finished laying down the pattern, cut the head while letting it rest in its cradle.

When finished the head should look like this.

Carving the Doll's Head

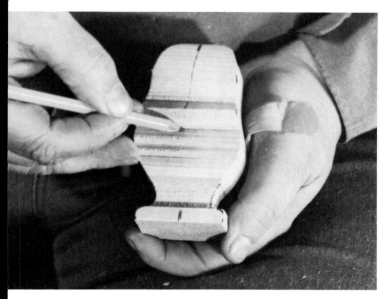

Begin by drawing a center line on the face.

Then mark a rough idea of the placement of the nose and eyes. Sometimes you will have the doll's expression clearly in mind before you start. Other times, it will evolve from the wood as you carve.

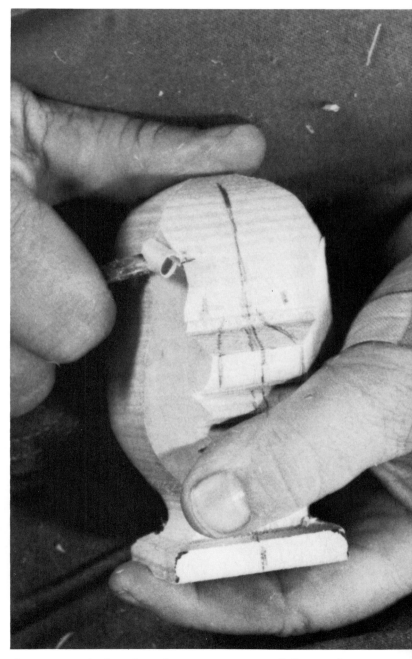

Start carving by knocking the square corners off all around.

Mark around the base, using your finger and the pencil as a compass. It is important to maintain the width of this base so the body will fit properly.

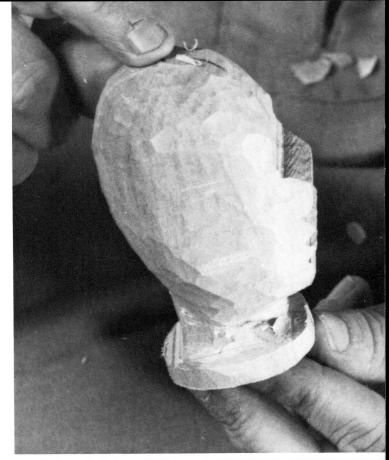

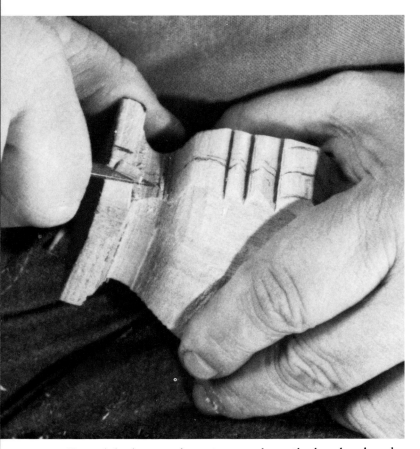

Round the base and continue to shape the head and neck.

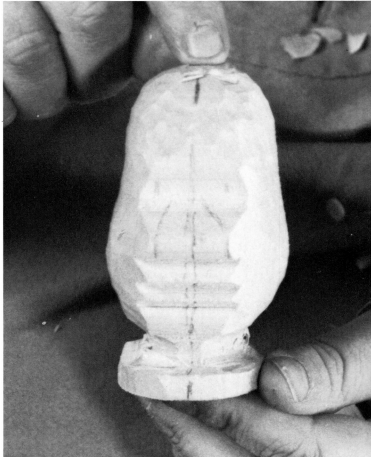

Before you do the face, the head should look like this.

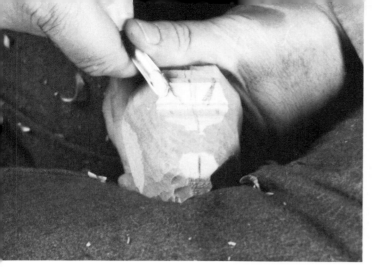

Use a gouge to remove wood beside the nose.

Make a stop cut up the lip toward the nostril.

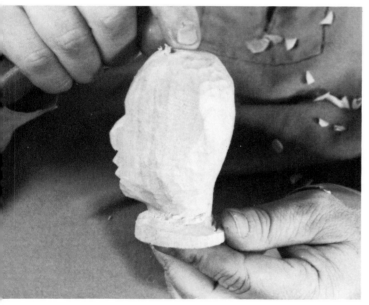

Shape the nose and carve the eye sockets.

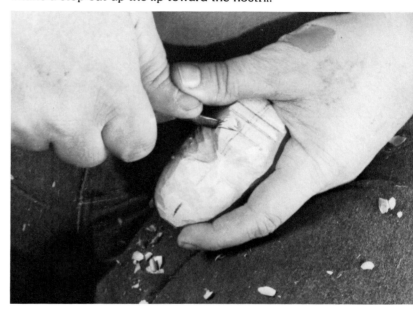

Trim back to the stop cut, rounding the underside of the nose.

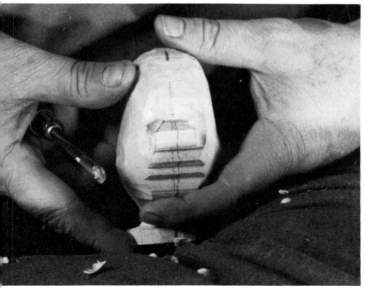

Leave the nose plenty wide at this point so you have enough to work with later.

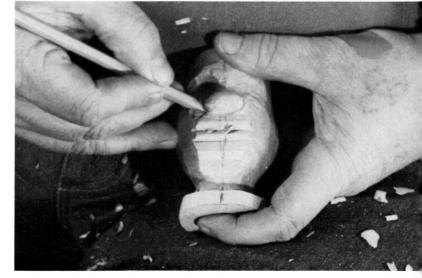

Mark the side of the mouth and the cheek line from the nostril to the corner of the mouth.

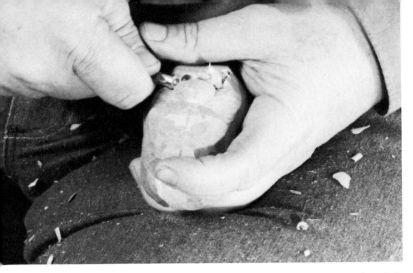

Use a gouge to cut the line. I use a gouge a lot on the doll project because it gives smoother lines.

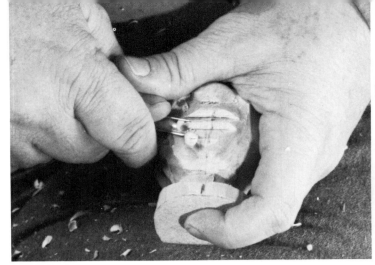

Gouge out the space between the lower lip and the chin.

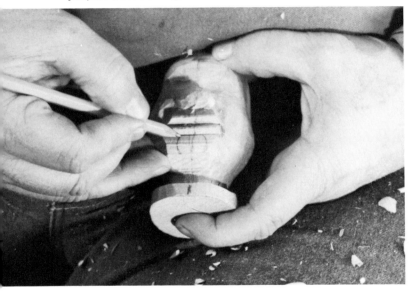

Mark the chin...

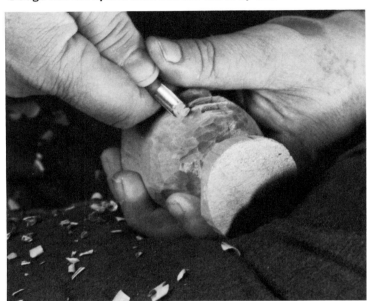

Take a bit more off the corners of the mouth.

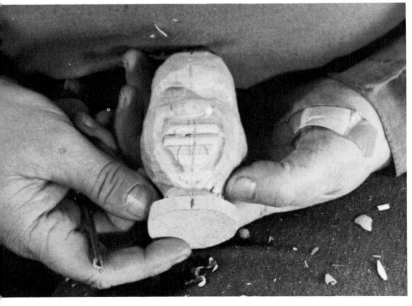

and carry the cheek lines down to it.

Refine the face.

Using a turned down blade, cut into the corner of the nose to get the curl of the nostril.

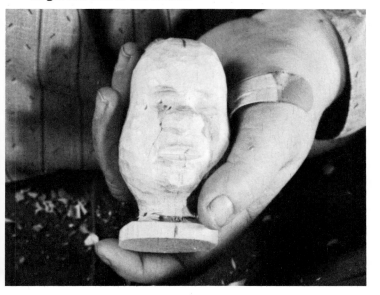

It's beginning to look like a face now.

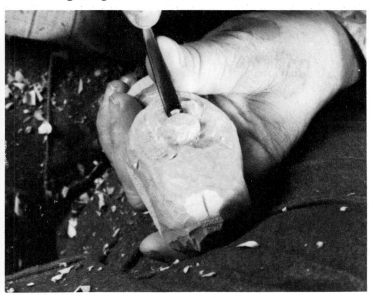

Use a gouge to make the "angel's fingerprint" between the upper lip and the nose.

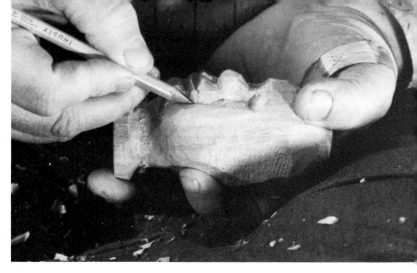

Mark in the shape of the mouth. The smile will come mostly from the cheeks so don't give the mouth too much of a turn. The lower lip will be a little shorter than the top, giving the doll a puckered, childlike look.

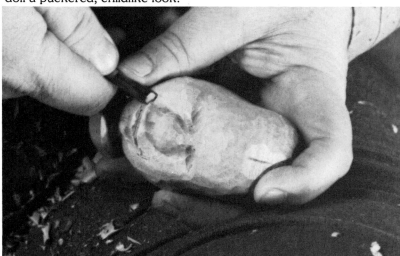

Carve the mouth.

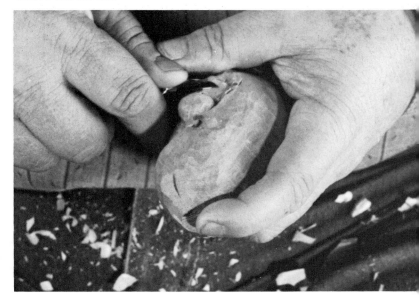

The eyebrows are rounded out. Heavier eyebrows have the effect of aging the figure.

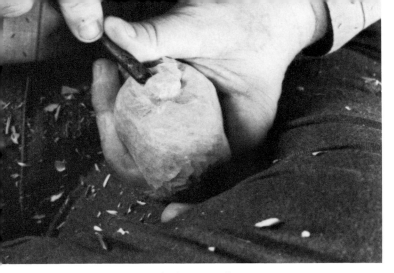

With the gouge mark the nostrils.

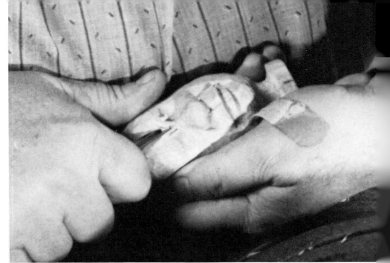

Carve a slight indentation between the eyes. This will accentuate the eyes.

Clean out the excess with a knife.

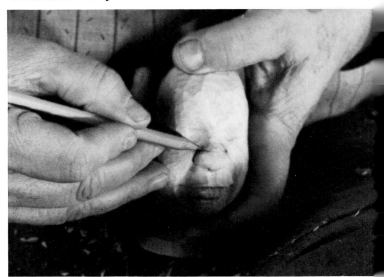

Mark over the nostril. This line will give it a flaring effect.

Look at your doll. On this model it appeared too squarish, so I trimmed the back of the head.

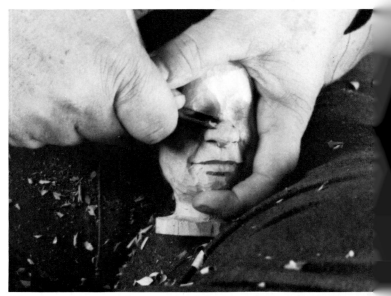

Use a gouge to cup the outside of the nostril. I usually finish the right side first and use it as a guide so the left side will be balanced.

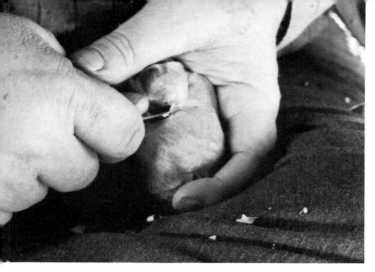

As you see things that need work do them. In this model the eye socket needed a little work.

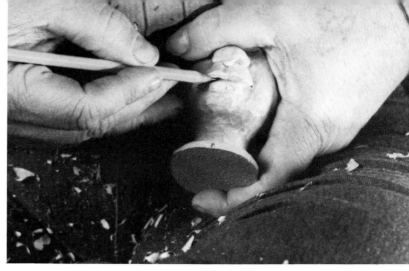

Open the mouth a little to reveal a little of the teeth. This gives the doll character.

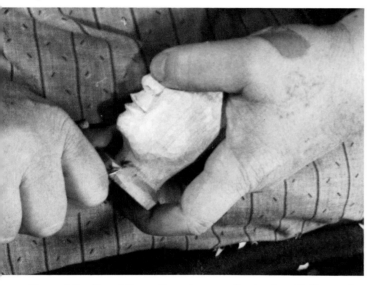

Round the lip of the collar piece so the body will fit evenly.

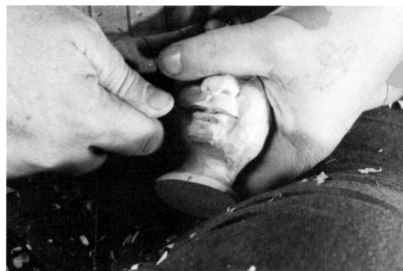

Use a sharp knife and try to do this in one clean cut. The less cuts, the smoother the result.

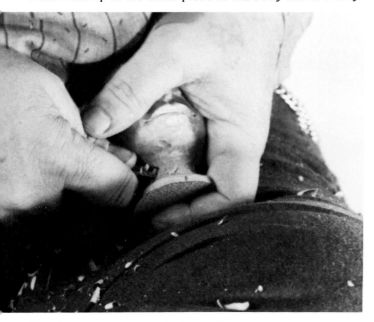

Use the gouge to smooth the neck.

You are trying to open a small flat place that will represent the teeth. I will make two teeth in this doll. The more teeth you have, the meaner the doll will look.

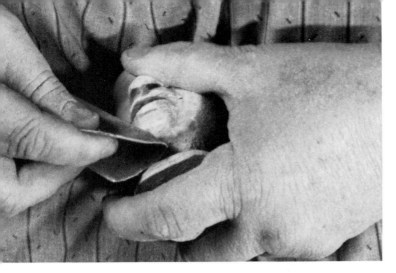

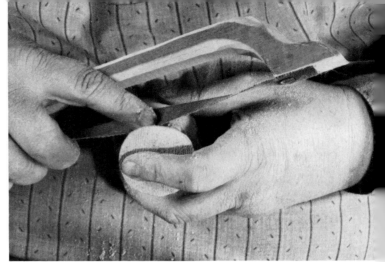

Using fine or extra fine paper, sand the head to make it smooth. In some carvings the carving marks give character, but because this is a young person, you'll want it smooth. This is much harder for me to do than an adult.

Use the fiddle-bow sander (see box) to cover large areas quickly.

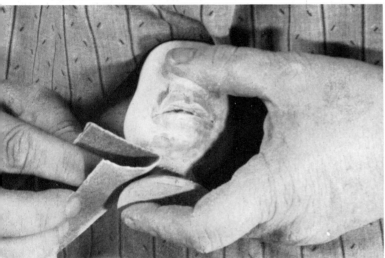

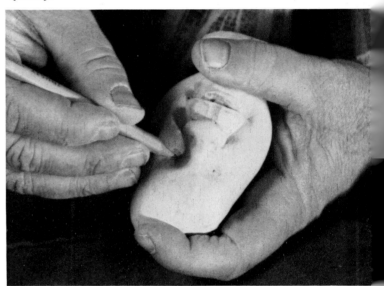

Cup and bend the sandpaper to get in the grooves. Sometimes it is necessary to fold the paper to a finer crease to get into certain spots.

When you've finished sanding, mark the center of the eyes at equal distances from the sides of the nose.

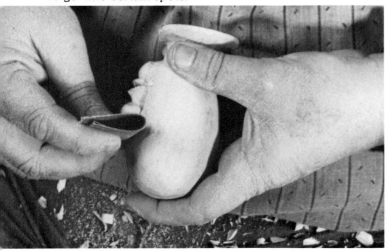

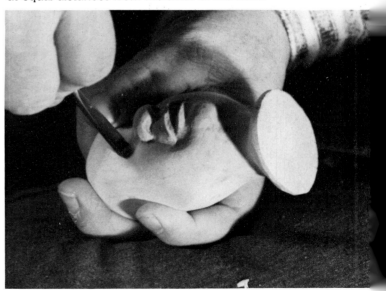

Whenever you sand, you will find places that are out of balance or need refinement. You have a different perspective and can catch things you missed while carving.

With a round gouge, mark the top edge of the eye.

MAKING A FIDDLEBOW SANDER

This helpful tool is easy to make and is invaluable in the sanding process of the doll and other projects. While it might seem new, it has probably been around for thousands of years, in one form or another. It is made from a piece of wood, usually cherry or maple for their hardness, cut in the shape of a fiddlebow. A pattern is included on the pattern pages. For paper I use a sandpaper belt cut apart or, when I can find it, sandpaper that comes in a long roll instead of a sheet.

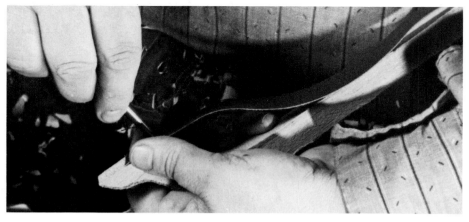

fasten the sandpaper to each end of the sander, putting screws in the pilot holes.

Using a piece about 1″ thick, trace the pattern and cut the shape out on the bandsaw.

Round off the edges...

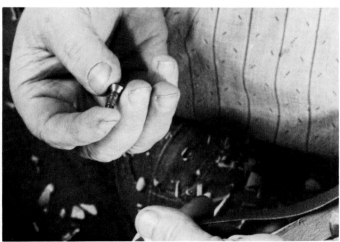

Drill pilot holes at each end of the sander. Cut apart a sandpaper belt so it is one straight piece, and cut off enough to stretch from one end of the fiddlebow to the other. Using heavy short screws...

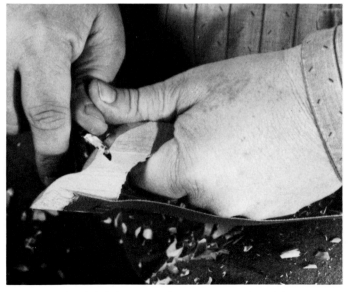

to make the fiddlebow sander more comfortable to your hand.

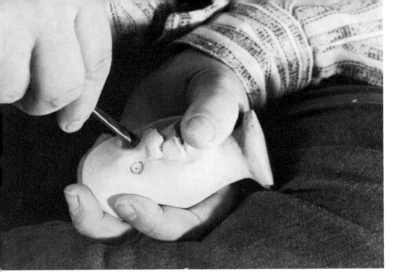

Do the same at the bottom.

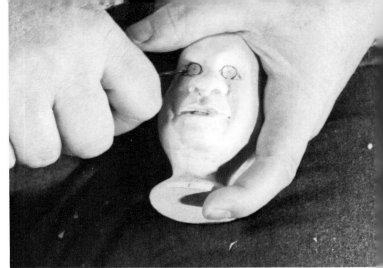

Do the same thing on the smaller, inside corners to arrive at this look.

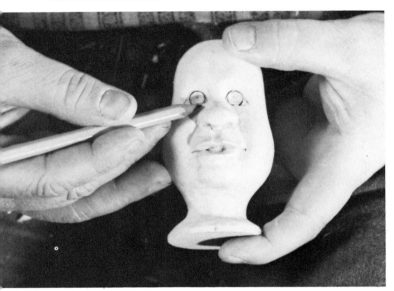

Mark the corners of the eyes.

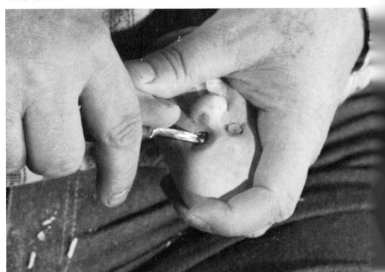

Round out the iris portion of the eye.

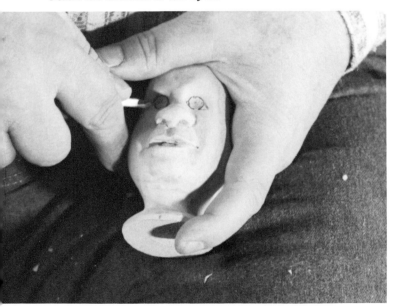

Use a thin turned-down knife to make a stop cut on one of the outside corner lines.

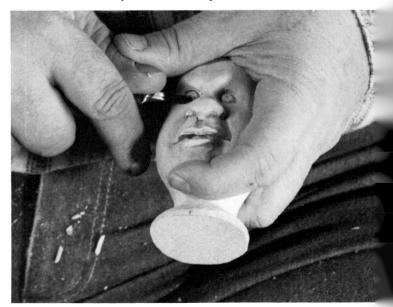

Go back and deepen this iris mark occasionally and round it out some more.

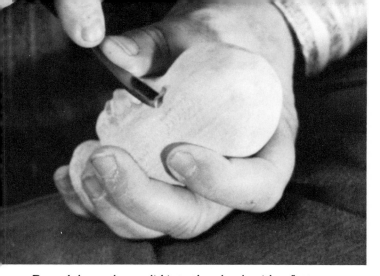

Round down the eyelid into the cheek with a flatter gouge.

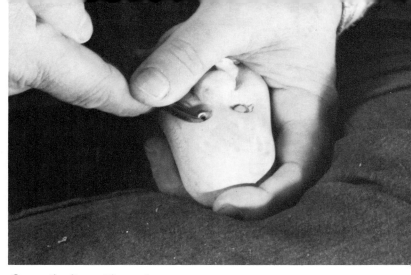

Score the line with a veiner.

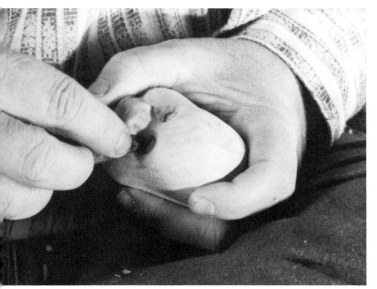

Clean up around the eye with 220-grit sandpaper, folding it until it fits where you want it.

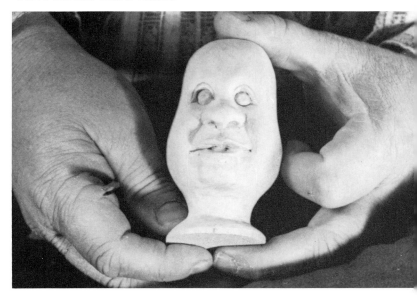

The face looks like this, needing only the pupils for finishing.

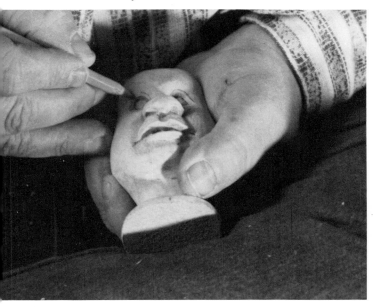

Mark the upper eyelid.

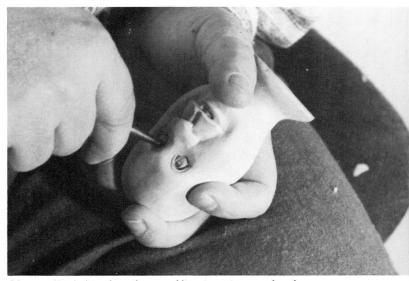

Use a 4/32 (⅛) inch nailset and line it up just under the upper eyelid. This will give an upward glance to the doll. When properly positioned push and turn the nailset to make the pupil. Do the same with both eyes.

Carving the Hands

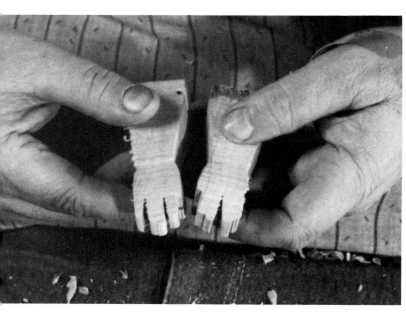

The two hands are similar but different enough to add character to the doll.

then on the palm. Mark the wood to be removed.

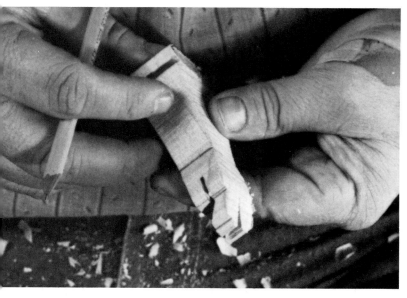

Mark the thumb in the left hand, first on the top...

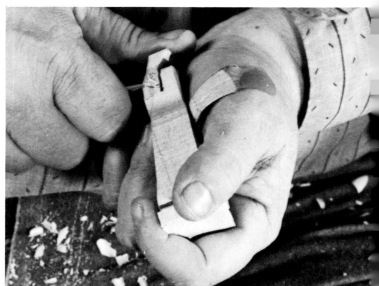

Trim the forefinger...

and the palm to make the thumb distinct.

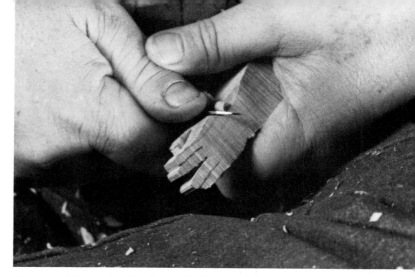

Round off the wrist, leaving it thick enough for a plump look.

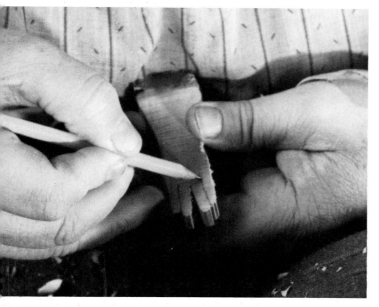

Mark the other finger, doing the outside first.

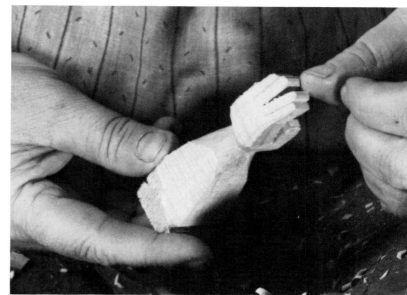

When the wrist is defined, it is a good time to round up the forearm.

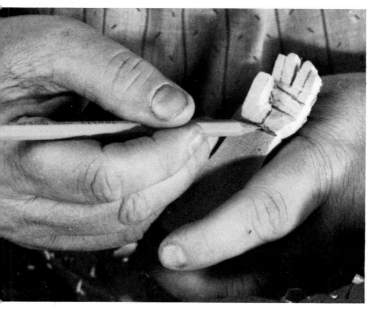

Then mark the inside, including the heel and wrist lines.

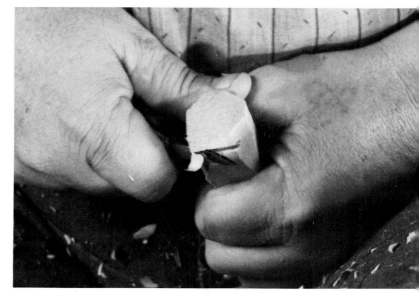

Begin by rounding the square corners.

25

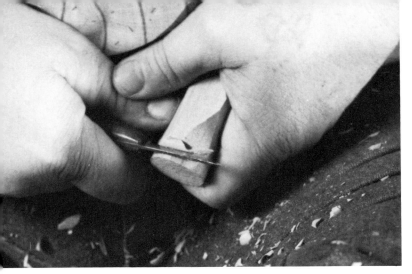

Continue the notch made with the bandsaw at the end of the arm all around it. This will be used to attach the cloth arm of the doll's body.

Round the heel of the hand.

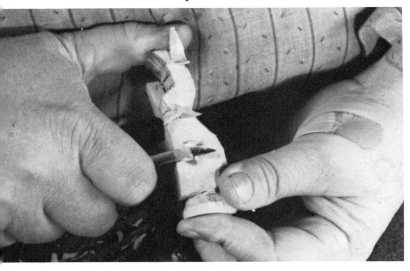

Round the forearm...

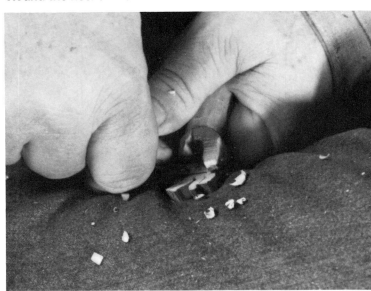

Score the hand and finger lines with a veiner.

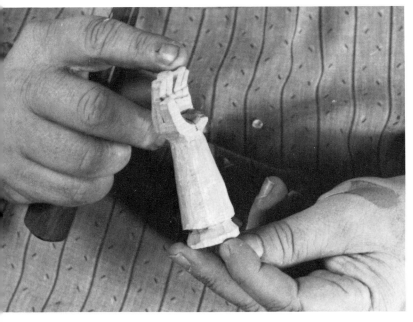

until you arrive at this basic shape.

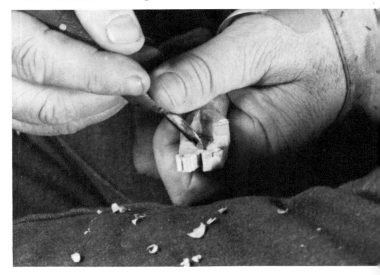

You may want to deepen and emphasize the lines between the fingers. You want them to come down to the callous line, but you don't want to over cut. This hand position will give you better control as you carve.

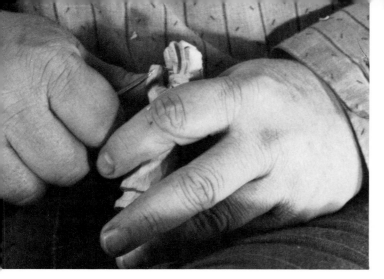

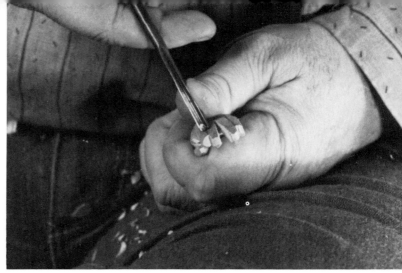

You want to round the fingers while leaving them thick enough for strength.

Use a veiner to separate the fingers, and a gouge to make depressions between the knuckles of the hand.

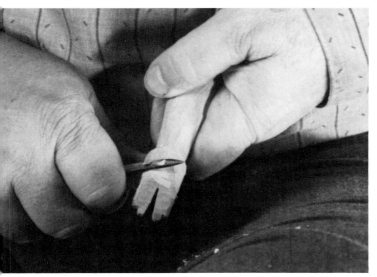

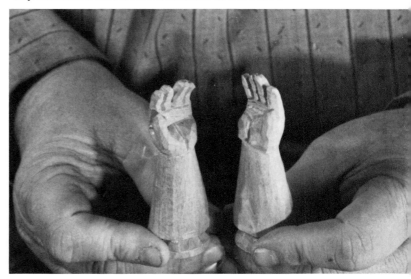

Flatten the back of the hand.

Follow the same steps on the other hand. When you are finished they should look like this...

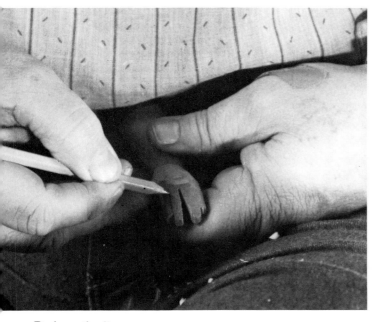

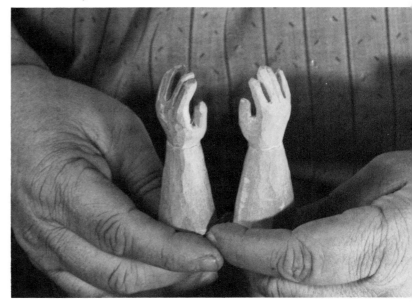

Redraw the lines.

and this...

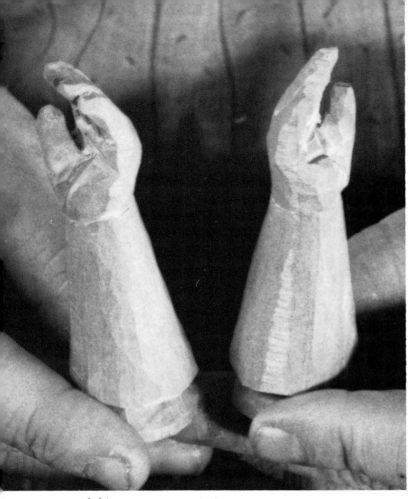

and this.

Use 220-grit sandpaper sheets for the more delicate work.

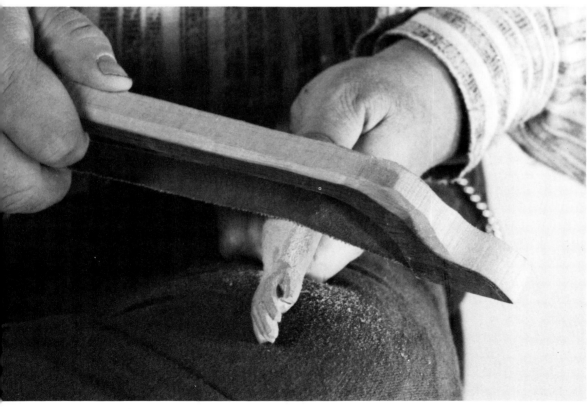
Use the fiddlebow sander to smooth the arms.

Carving the Feet

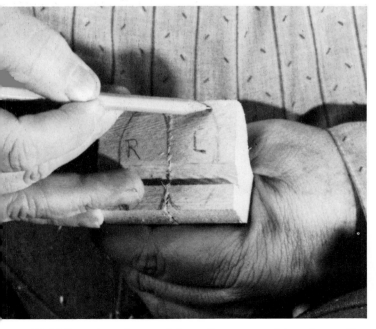

Since the blanks for the feet are identical, begin by marking them left and right.

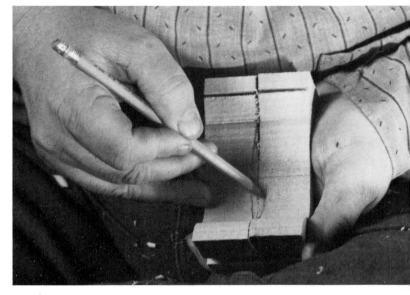

Still holding the legs together, turn to the front and draw the inside lines of the calves.

Hold them together and draw the appropriate sole profile.

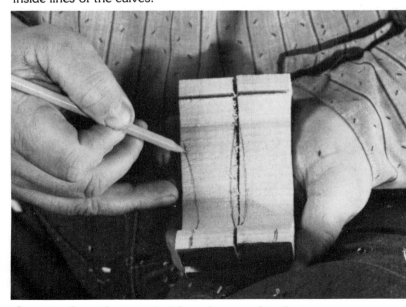

Carrying the widest point of the sole around to the toe, use it as a guide for beginning the line for this outside of the calves.

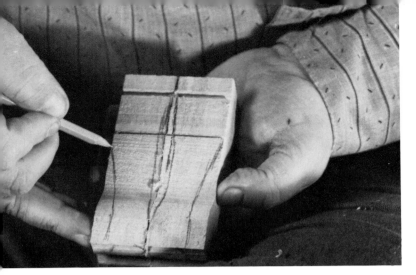

Draw similar lines on the back of the boots.

Make a slight curve on the instep.

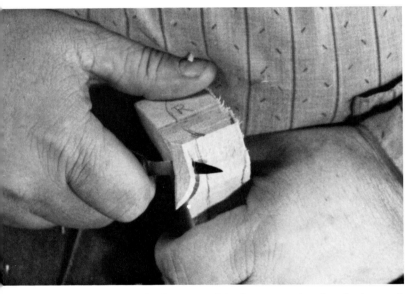

Beginning at the bottom of the leg, start shaping the leg and foot. Carve down the leg toward the shoe to get the indentation at the ankle.

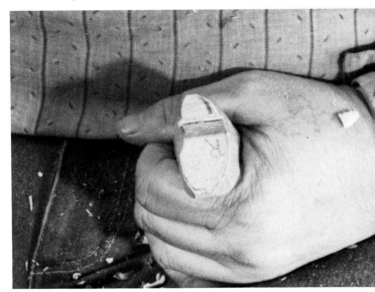

Trim the bottom of the foot making the heel narrower than a man's shoe would be.

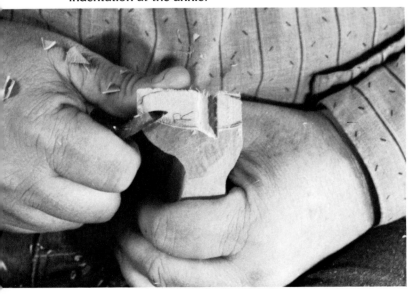

Round the foot.

Round the top, beginning with the corners.

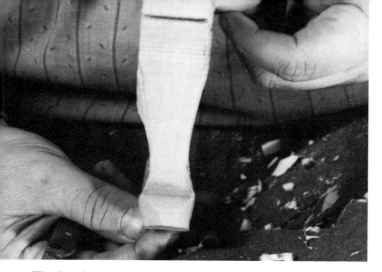

The leg should be shaped something like this. At the knee it will be thicker than it is wide.

Cut a stop directly into the line...

Round the corners at the top of the leg.

and carve down to it.

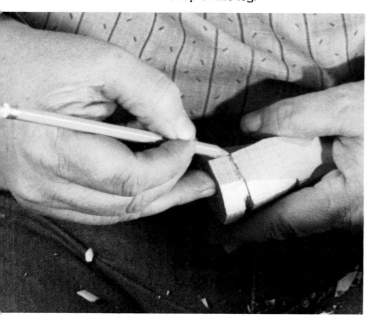

Mark the notch around.

The top will look like this. Continue to round the calf.

A REPAIR TIP

As we carved the leg we found a crack in the wood. Instead of starting over we made a simple repair.

First, gently stick your knife in the crack and open it up a bit.

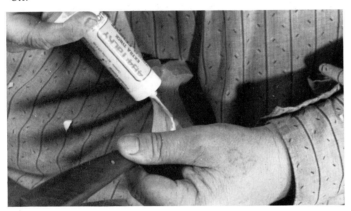

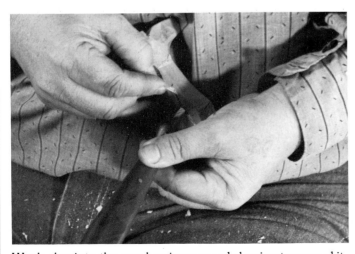

Work glue into the crack using a wood shaving to spread it in.

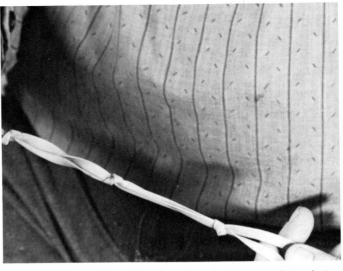

Loop several strong rubber bands together to make a chain.

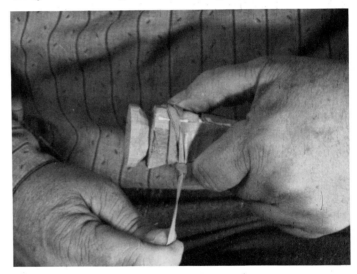

Holding an end against the piece wrap the chain of rubber bands tightly around it.

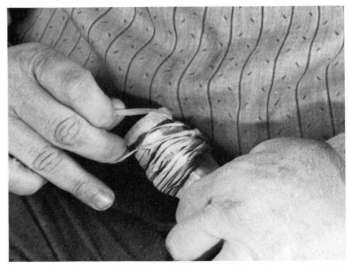

Loop the other end of the chain around the piece and let it sit until it dries.

Draw the top of the boot angling down from front to back.

Cut down the calf to the boot stop all around.

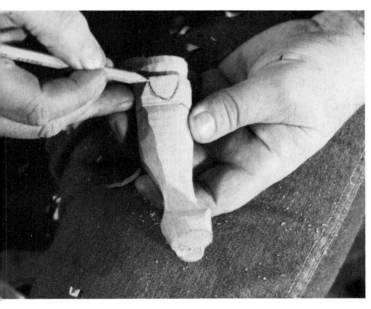

Draw in the knee cap.

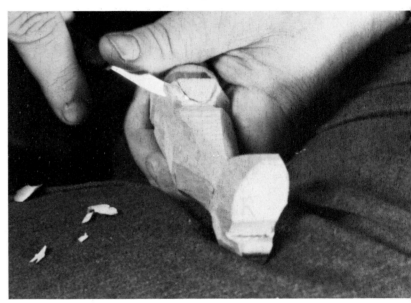

Trim around the knee cap with small curl cuts.

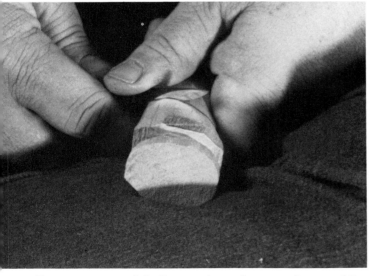

Cut a stop around the line you have drawn at the top of the boot.

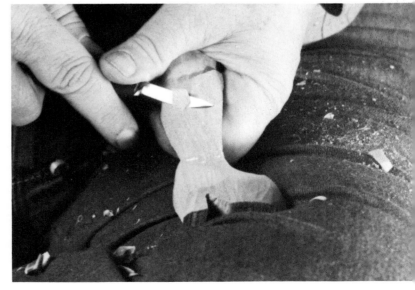

Flatten and refine the surfaces.

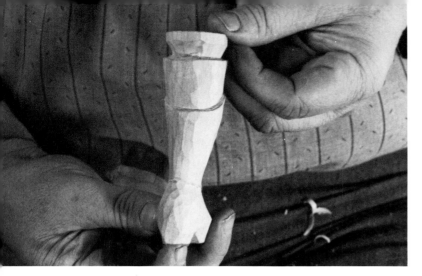

The back of the leg should look like this.

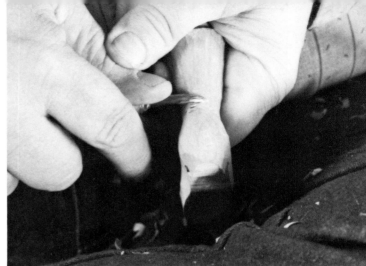

Make stop cuts and chip out the wood.

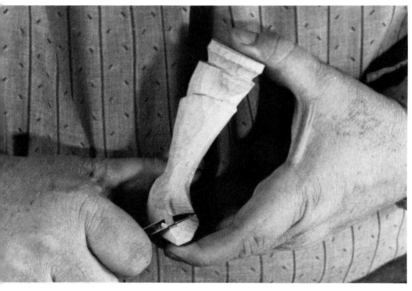

Round the toe of the boot and the rest of the shoe area.

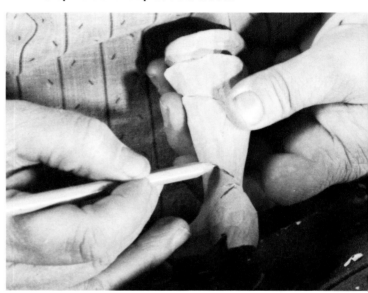

On both sides of the back of the boot mark a "V" pointing back.

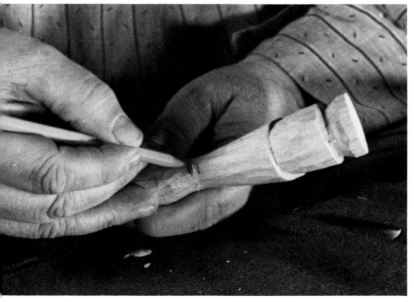

Mark folds around the ankle area. These small notches give the boot a realistic look.

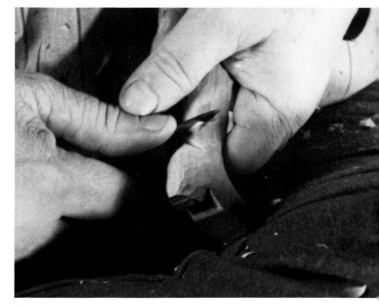

Cut them out.

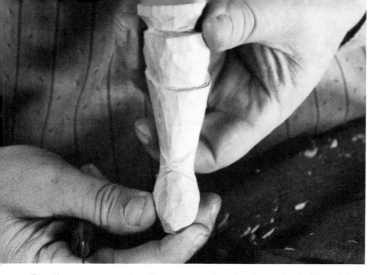

Do the same on the front to make the boot look like this.

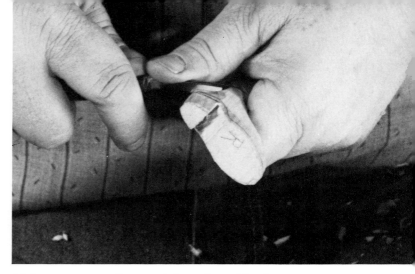

Make a stop cut all around the sole and heel.

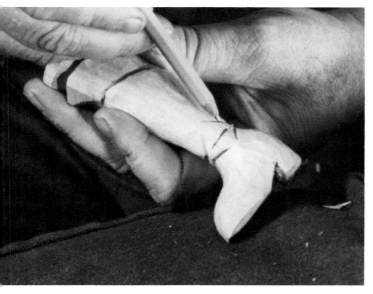

Mark a line on the sides of each boot and notch out as above.

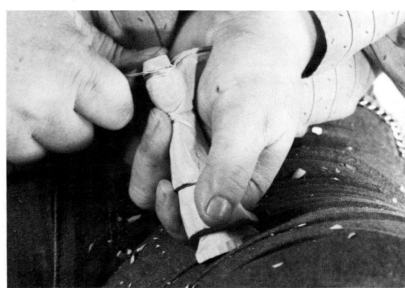

Make very small, very careful cuts all around the boot to the sole and heel.

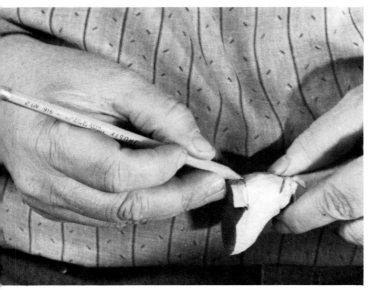

Draw a line around the sole and heel. Use your finger as a depth gauge.

Draw a line down the outside of the boot where it will fasten. The line should go straight down the side, turning toward the toe at the ankle.

To make the eyes of the boot use a half-round gouge. Place the open corners of the "U" on the line with the cup behind the line. Push and rock the gouge.

Use a small turned down knife and notch out an area around the scallop. This will make the back of the boot appear to go under the front, "eyed" part.

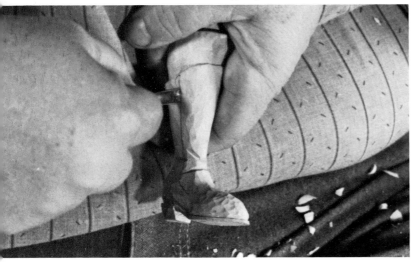

Make the next gouge mark right next to the first and continue down the leg.

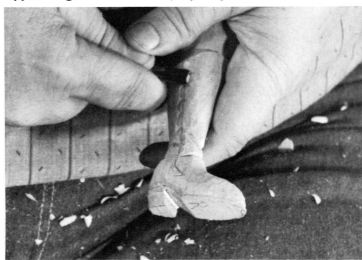

Use a gouge to make a button hole dent in each scallop.

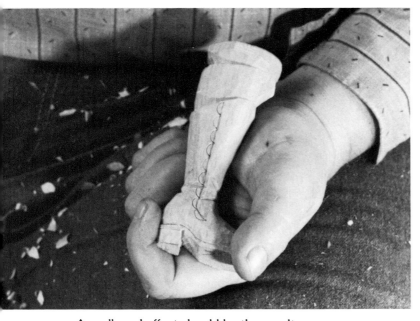

A scalloped effect should be the result.

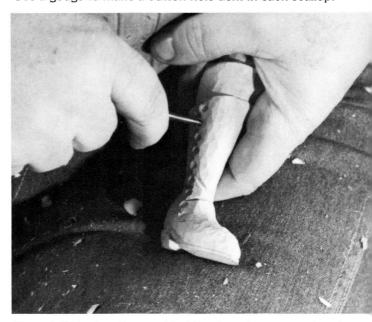

Use a 3/32 inch nailset and holding it at the center of each scallop push, rock, roll and turn it to make a button.

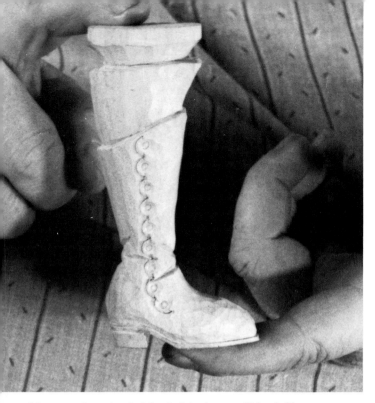

Here is what the finished right boot will look like.

Sand the boot with the fiddlebow sander...

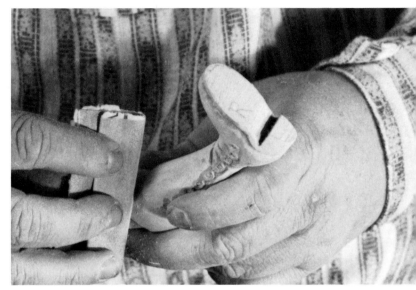

and folded 220-grit sandpaper. When everything is sanded you are ready to move on to the painting of the doll.

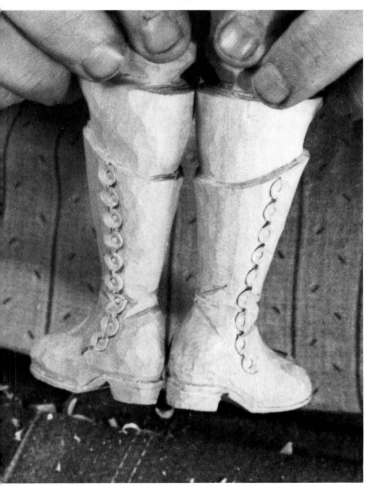

Do the same thing on the left, being certain to have the buttons on the outside.

Directions for painting are found in the color section of this book.

The Doll's Body and Clothing

Tools: Pins

Tracing Paper (14" x 17" available at Arts

Black Sharpie™ Marker: Extra fine point permanent marker by Sanford

Pencil

Scissors

Fabric Pen (Mark-B-Gone™ made in Japan)

Sewing Machine

Ruler

Tacky Glue: comes in a bottle or hypodermic applicator. Will not run. Hot glue will damage the doll's wig.

Materials: 1/3-1/2 yard 45" muslin for the body

1 spool Button and carpet thread

3/4 yard print fabric for the dress (It should be a small print or plaid in light colors. No dark colors or big prints.)

1 spool Thread to match fabric

1/2 yard solid or print fabric for the pinafore

1/3-1/2 yard white fabric for the bloomers

1/2 yard

1/4" flat lace for bloomers and the neck of the dress

1/2 yard, 1/2" ruffled lace for the arms of the pinafore

1 yard, 1" flat lace for the bottom of the pinafore

1 yard, 3/8" ribbon for pinafore ties

2 yards, 1/4" elastic

1 bag polyester stuffing

1 pack snaps or Velcro for closing the back of the dress and pinafore

1 doll's wig

1 doll stand

(Note: Wigs and stands are available at most doll stores or from: Bell Ceramics, Inc. P.O. Box 127 Dept. B-432 Clermont, Florida 32711 or Doll Parts Supply Co. 5-15 49th Ave. Long Island City, NY 11101

The Patterns

On the following pages you will find the patterns for the doll body and dress. Lay the tracing paper over the patterns and trace them with a pencil. When you have a good copy, remove the tracing paper from the page and go over your lines with the black "Sharpie" Marker. Be sure all the marks and directions are accurately copied on each pattern piece, as well as the piece's name. then cut each pattern piece from the tracing paper.

When you finish laying out the patterns and cutting the fabric, you should have the following pieces for the doll.

The body: 2 trunk pieces, front and back

2 arms

2 legs

The bloomers: 2 parts

The dress: 1 front

2 backs

2 sleeves

1 facing

1 skirt

1 ruffle

The pinafore: 2 front top pieces

4 back top pieces

1 skirt

2 waistbands

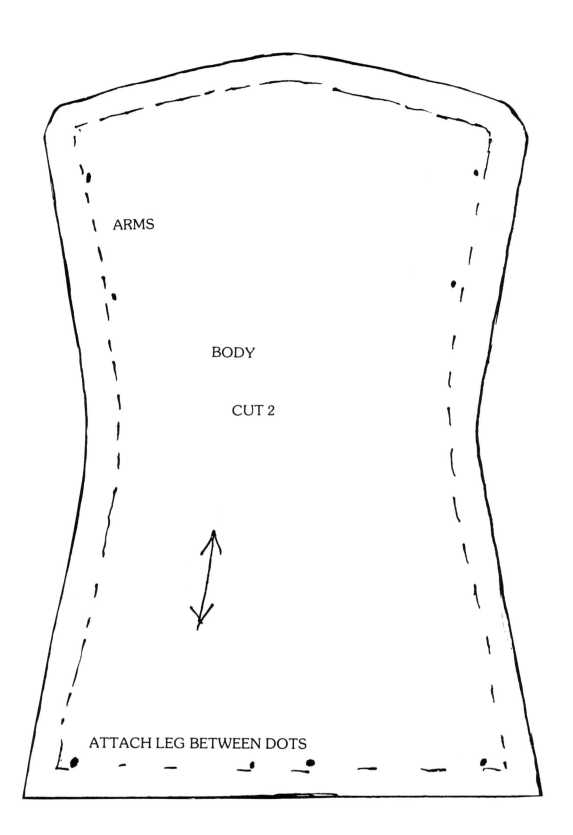

ARMS

BODY

CUT 2

ATTACH LEG BETWEEN DOTS

ARM

CUT 2

LEG

CUT 2

40

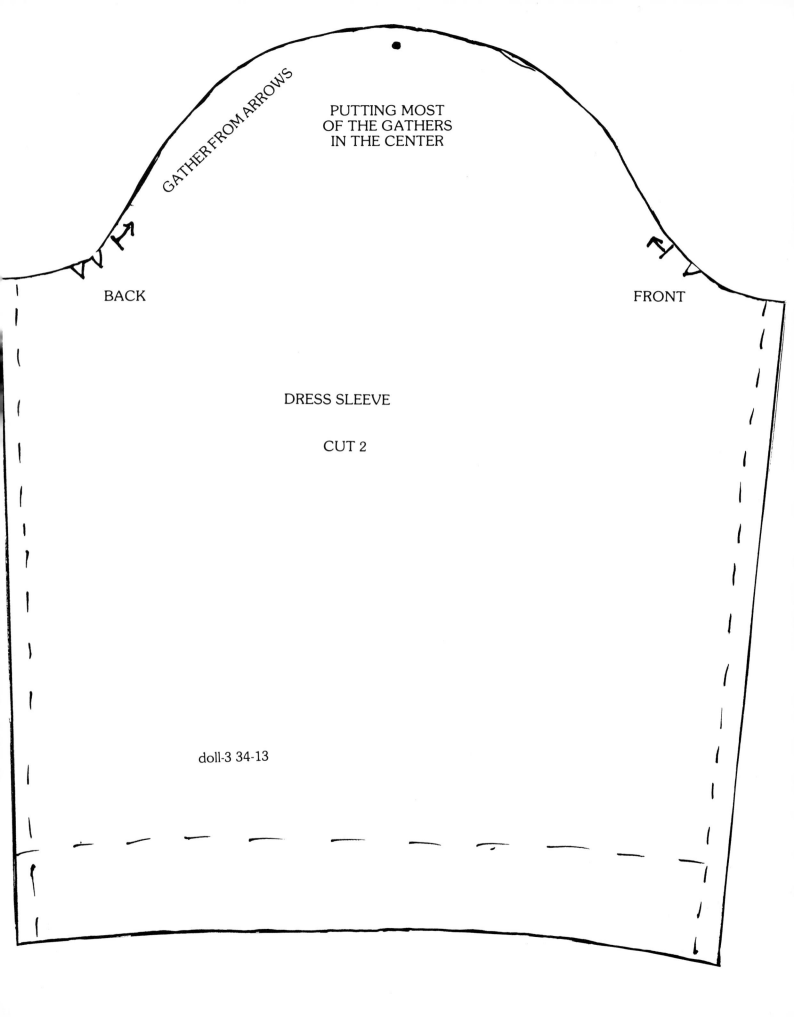

GATHER FROM ARROWS

PUTTING MOST
OF THE GATHERS
IN THE CENTER

BACK

FRONT

DRESS SLEEVE

CUT 2

doll-3 34-13

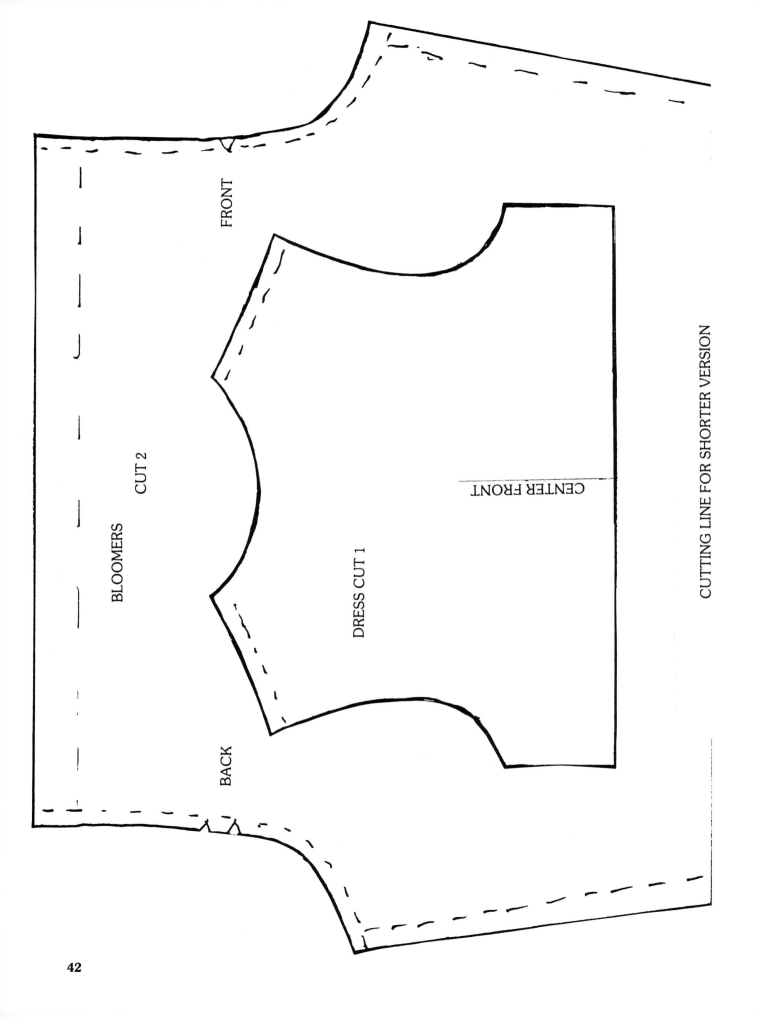

FRONT

BLOOMERS CUT 2

DRESS CUT 1

CENTER FRONT

BACK

CUTTING LINE FOR SHORTER VERSION

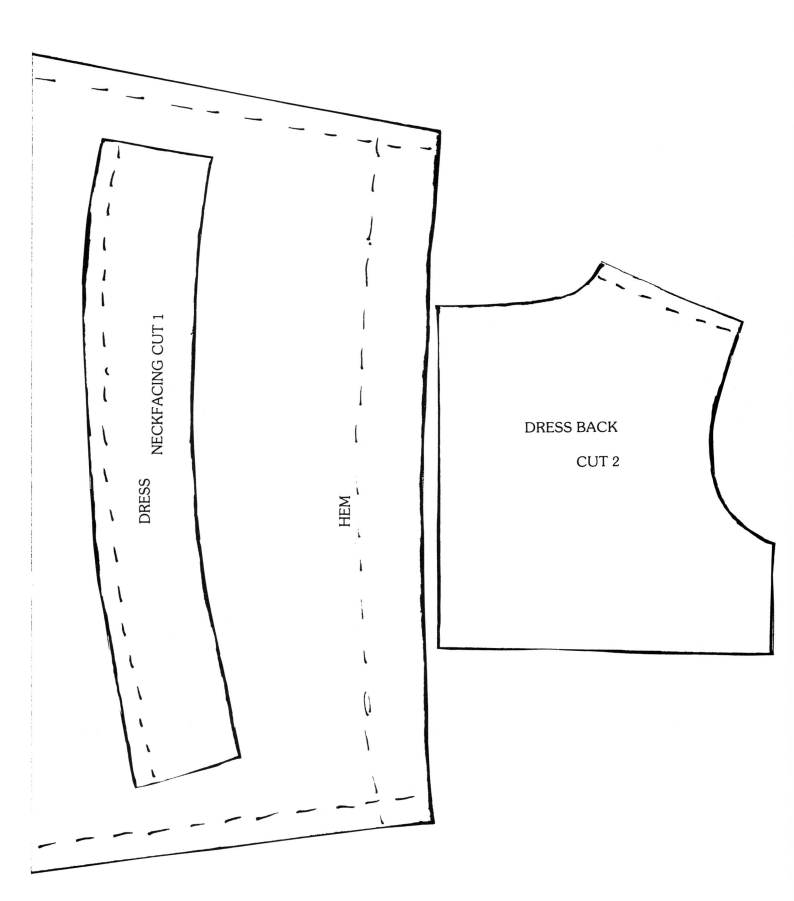

DRESS NECKFACING CUT 1

DRESS

HEM

DRESS BACK

CUT 2

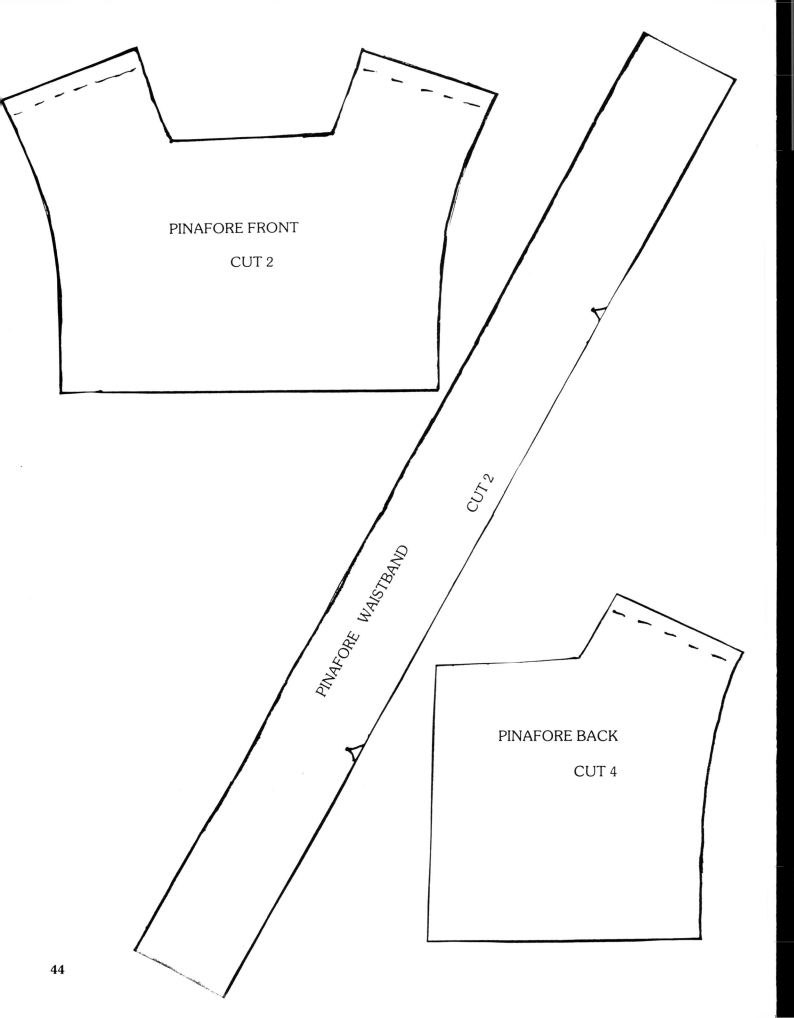

PINAFORE FRONT

CUT 2

PINAFORE WAISTBAND

CUT 2

PINAFORE BACK

CUT 4

44

MAKING ALTERATIONS

There may be a need to change the size of the doll. Alterations to the pattern are simple. To make things smaller you simply cut a pattern piece in half, overlap the halves and tape. To make things larger, again cut the pattern, separate the pieces to the desired size, fill in the gaps with paper and tape.

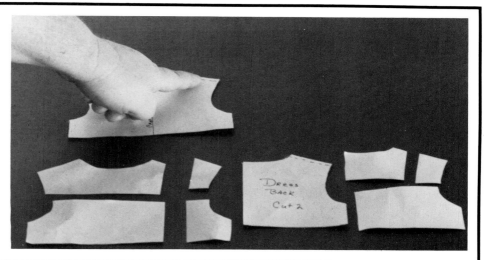

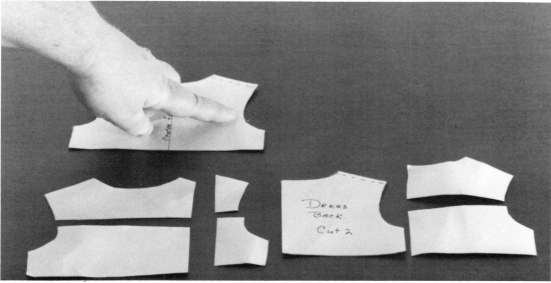

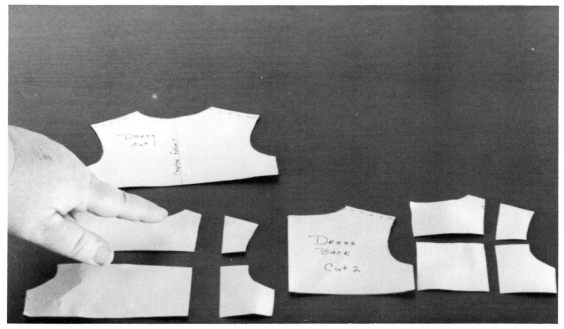

To make any change in the front and back parts of the dress top, larger or smaller, you must cut in these places.

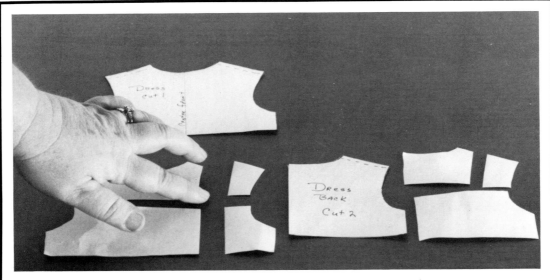

For example, if the shoulder is too narrow you can make it wider by cutting where I am pointing and spread it out as I have below.

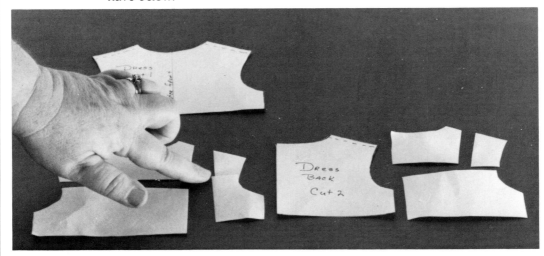

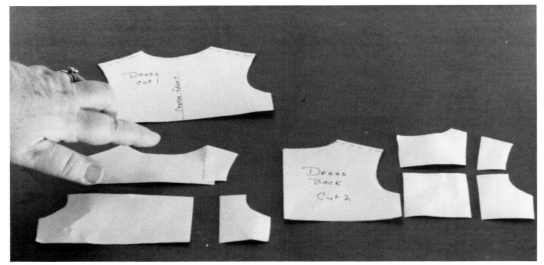

To make the pieces smaller you would overlap them as here and tape them. Be sure to do the same thing to all parts of the pattern.

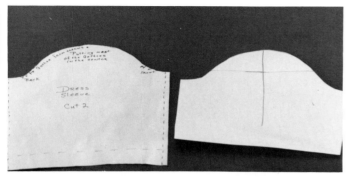

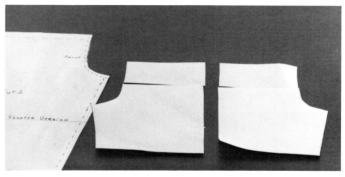

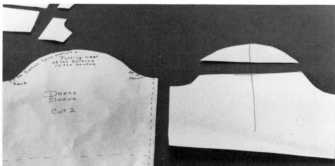

The bloomer will also need to be adjusted if you change the dress size. Cut the patterns where indicated.

If you make changes in the front and back parts you must then make the same changes in the sleeves. This is done by cutting the places marked in the photo.

To make the bloomers shorter, overlap the patterns like this.

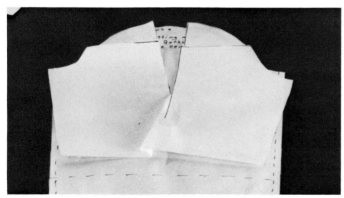

To make a fuller sleeve cut a line in the pattern and spread it to make a "V". Then add a piece to it.

To make them longer, separate the patterns as shown and add some extra paper to the pattern.

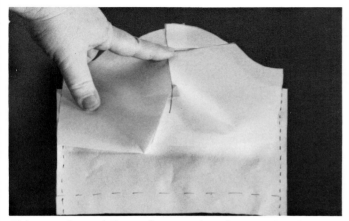

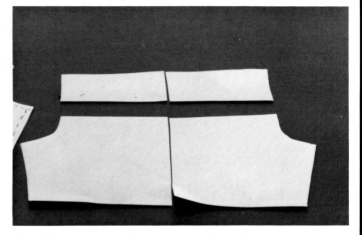

If the arm is too full, cut the same line, but overlap the sides and tape. The skirt may be adjusted by shortening or lengthening at the bottom.

The fullness of the bloomers may be adjusted in the same way.

Cutting the Fabric

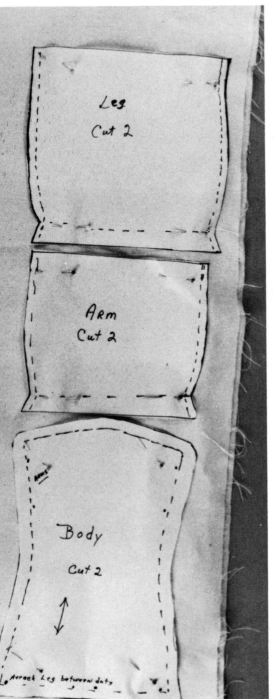

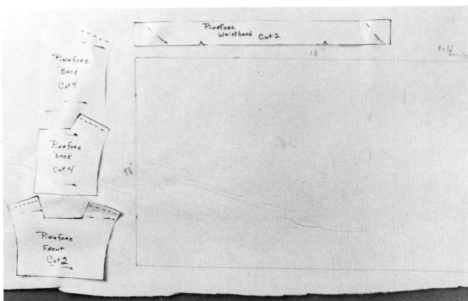

Fold the fabric for the pinafore in half. The main piece of the pinafore is a 9½″ x 30″ rectangle, but with the fold you can draw it 9½″ x 15″. From the fold measure 15″ over and draw a straight line. Then measure 9½ inches down and 15″ back to the fold. Lay the other pattern pieces around this rectangle. When you cut, do not cut the fold. When unfolded your rectangle will be 9½″ x 30″. This must be a single piece so be careful.

Lay the body patterns on a folded piece of muslin. Pin the pattern to the fabric being sure to go through both layers, then cut through both layers of fabric at the same time.

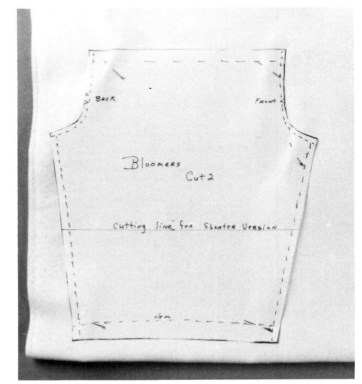

Fold the bloomer fabric in half. Lay the bloomer pattern on it, pin and cut.

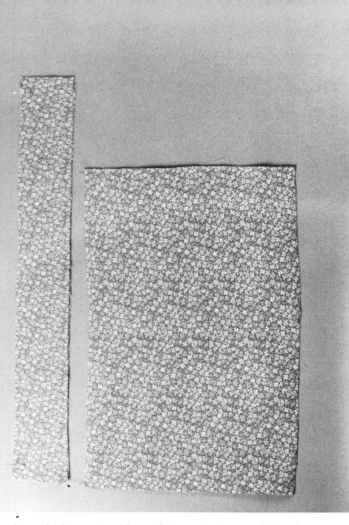

The next three rectangles are 9½" x 2½" with the 2½" side on the fold so they unfold to 19" x 2½". These are the ruffles of the dress. Lay the dress front and neckfacing beside the rectangles and cut all the pieces.

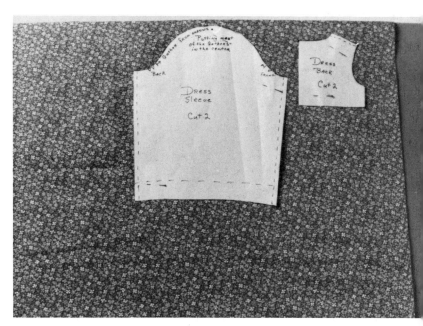

On the remaining fabric (still folded) lay the dress sleeve and dress back and cut out two of each. Save scraps of your fabric for a doll quilt.

Assembling the Body

The assembly of the body begins with the arms. Begin with the ¼" elastic and the arm pieces. Starting ½" from the end of the elastic mark two 2" lengths with ½" spaces in between as shown. Don't cut the elastic until after it is sewn in place.

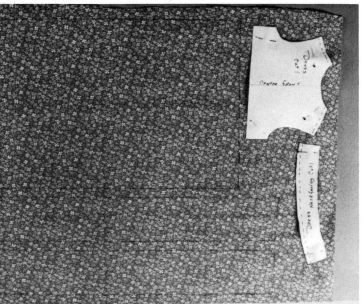

Fold the dress material in half so you have a piece about 21" (depending on the width of your fabric) x 27". Along the fold you will be marking four rectangles. You may measure them directly onto the fabric or cut paper patterns, which may be easier. The first will be 17" x 9" with the 9" side along the fold so it will open to 34" x 9". This is the skirt portion of the dress.

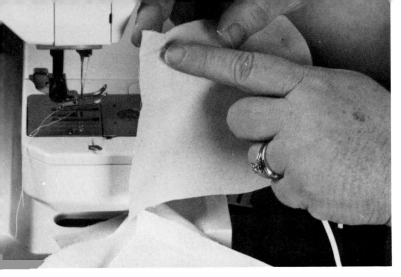

At the groove in the arm piece...

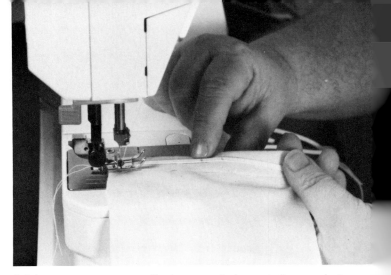

Make one or two small zig-zag stitches at the mark to secure the elastic.

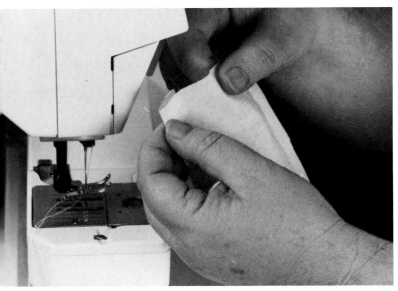

fold the fabric over.

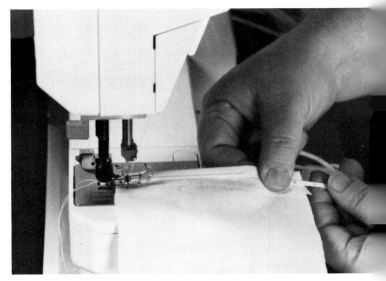

Being sure the piece is clamped into the sewing machine, stretch the elastic until the first 2" line is at the other edge of the arm.

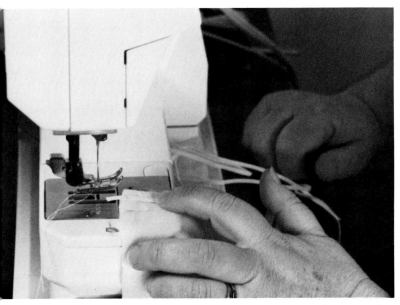

Lay the elastic over the fold so that the first mark is near the edge of the fabric.

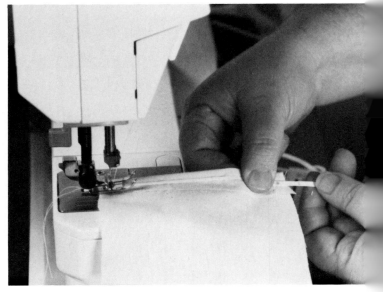

Maintaining the tension, sew the elastic to the arm piece.

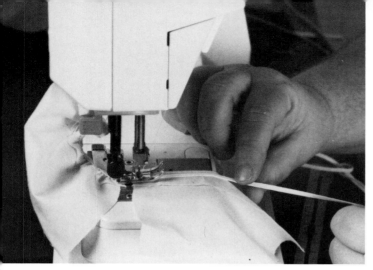

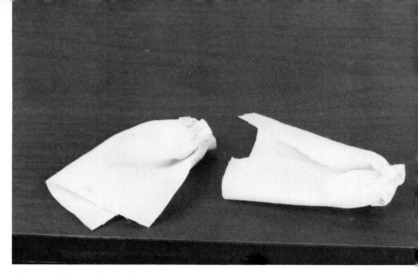

They will look like this.

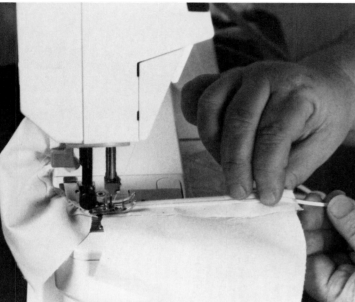

Without cutting, lay the other arm into position and follow the same steps. Sew a couple of stitches beginning at the mark, stretch the elastic until the next mark reaches the edge, then sew it down.

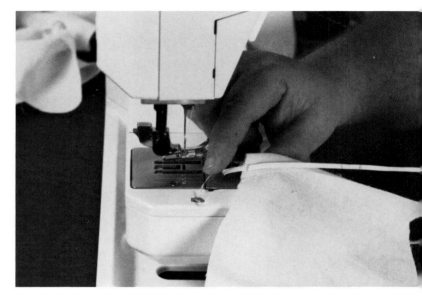

Follow the same steps with the legs, except make the elastic 2 ¼" between the dots.

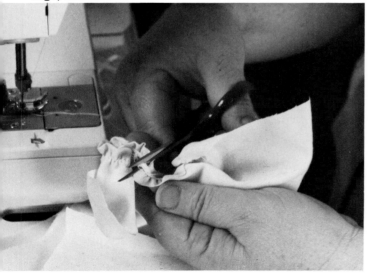

When both pieces are complete cut them apart.

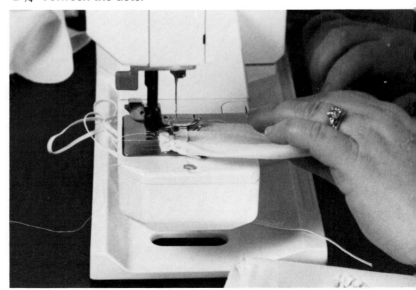

With the elastic side showing, use a straight stitch to sew a ¼" seam up the arms and legs.

Before turning them right-side out they will look like this.

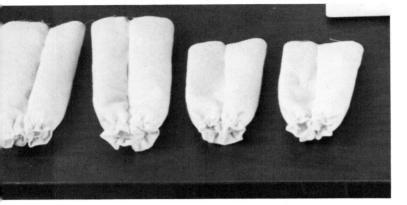

After turning them right-side out they will look like this. The seams will be at the back of the legs and arms.

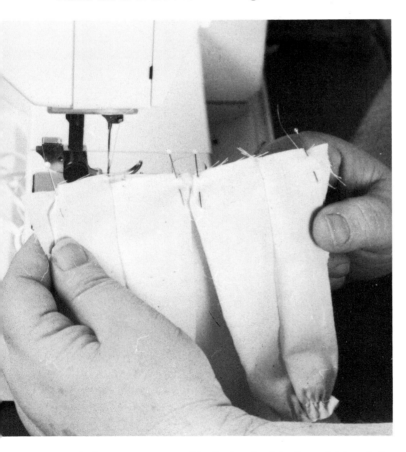

With the seam centered in the back of the legs, fold and pin tiny pleats at each corner where they will attach to the body. For an idea of the size of the pleats look at the body pattern.

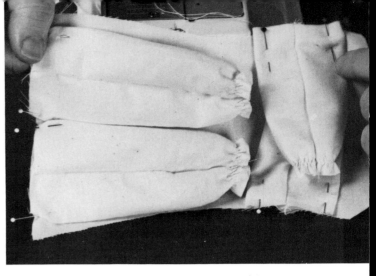

Pin the legs and arms to a body piece as shown.

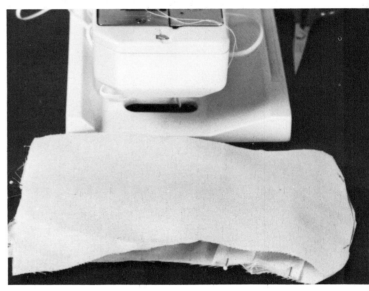

Lay the other body piece over the top and mark the space for the neck. You may wish to pin or baste these pieces together before sewing.

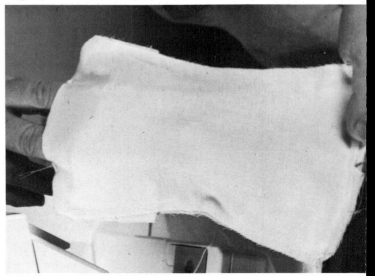

Beginning at one neck mark sew a ¼" seam all around the body to the other neck mark, to end up with this result.

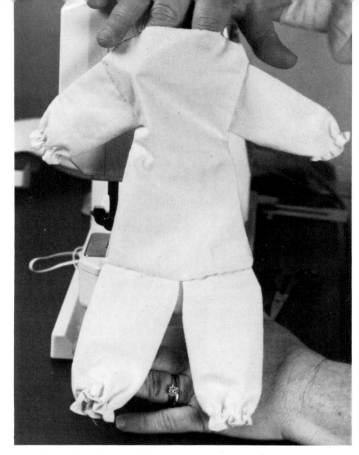

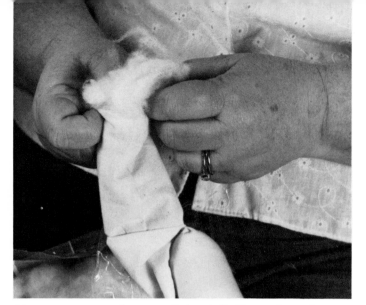

Turning things inside-out through the neck opening will give you this result. This is the front view, without arm or leg seams...

and this is the rear view.

You are now ready to stuff the doll. Using the polyester stuffing fill the body, arms and legs. You must stuff the body very tightly because of the weight of the head, hands and feet. Stuffing the doll tightly will also make it last longer. I was once told you stuff it until it's full, then you stuff it some more. You can use a dowel pin to tamp the stuffing tighter. Never use scissors. I use about 4 ounces of stuffing.

Start with the arms and legs...

then stuff the body. When the stuffing is complete, lay the body aside and finish the sewing.

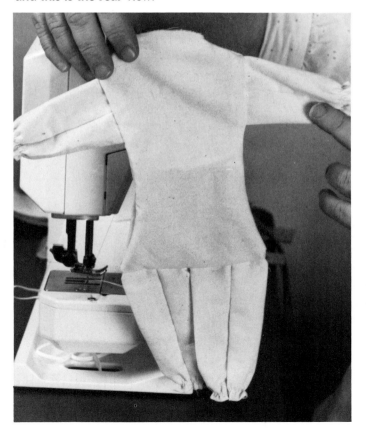

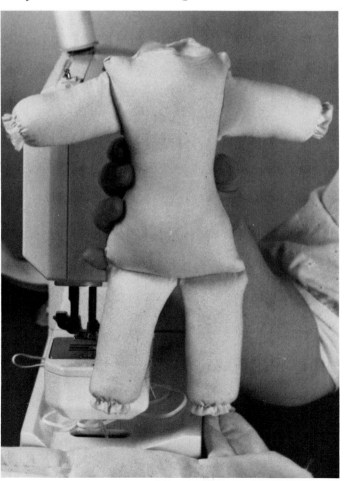

The Bloomers

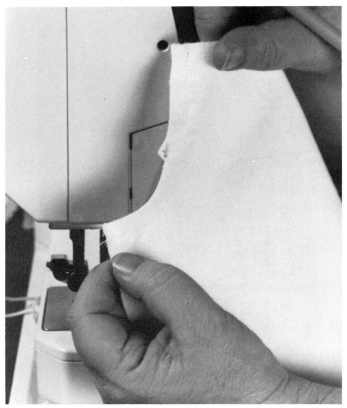

Match the front edges of the two bloomer pieces. The front of the crotch has a single notch. Match the notches and sew around the crotch.

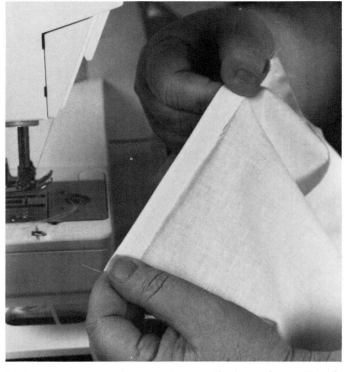

At the bottom of each piece, turn up the hem about ½″ and pin.

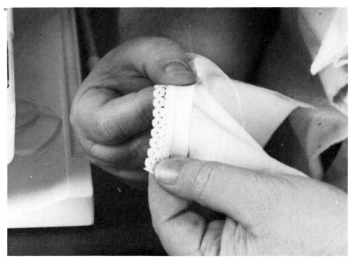

Sew a piece of ¼″ flat lace to the turned-up hem. Use a small zig-zag stitch.

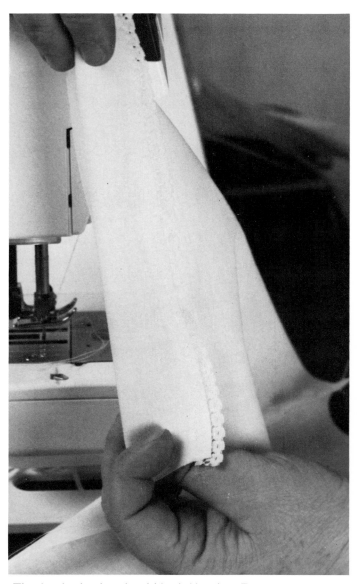

The finished sides should look like this. Front.

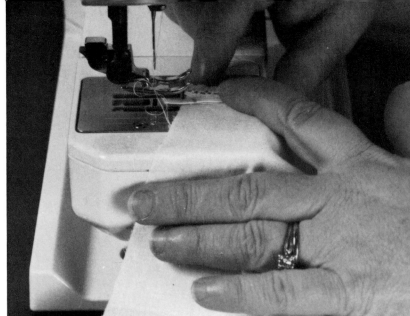

Line the first mark of the elastic just inside the edge of the fabric and tack it down.

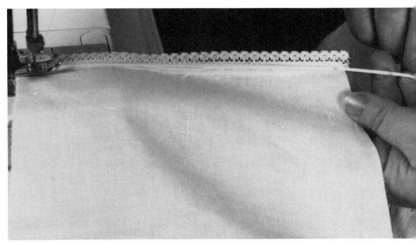

When it is securely fastened stretch the elastic until the next mark reaches the other edge.

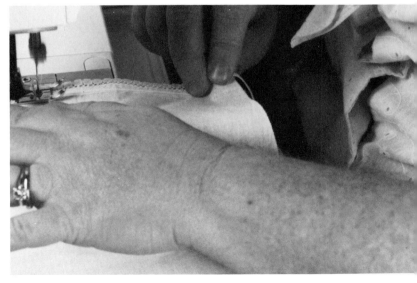

Sew in place with a zig-zag stitch.

Back.

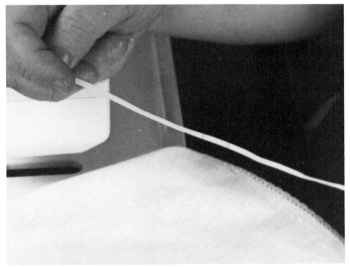

You are now going to sew the elastic on the legs of the bloomers. You will mark the elastic with the fabric pin as you did on the arms and legs of the body. Beginning ½" from the end of the elastic, mark two lengths 3" long with ½" in between. If you are making the shorter version mark these segments 3½" long.

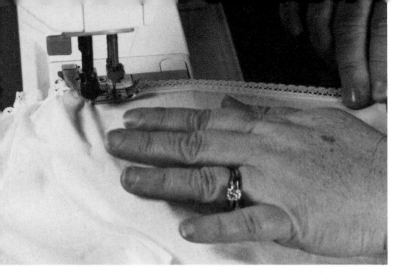

Without cutting the elastic, do the same on the other leg.

When complete the legs should look like this.

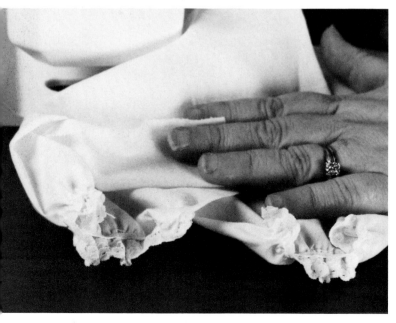

When both are finished cut the elastic.

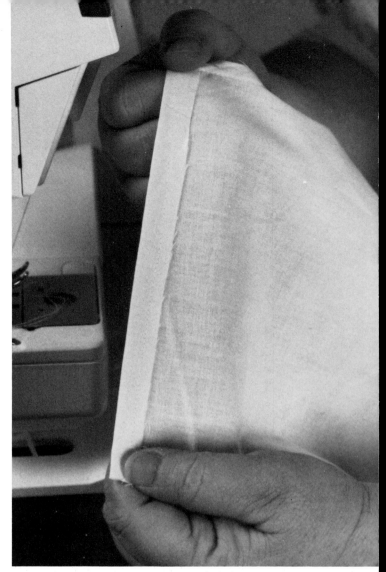

You do a similar thing with the waist. Turn down the top edge ½″ and sew with a regular straight stitch.

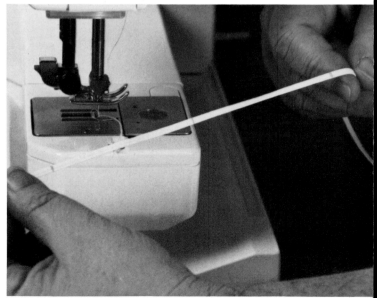

Take a piece of elastic 5¾ inches long and mark the beginning, middle and end of the elastic.

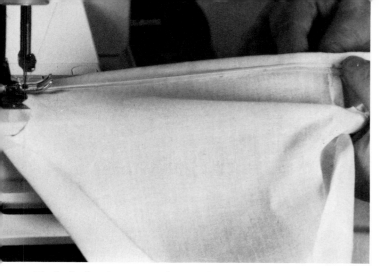

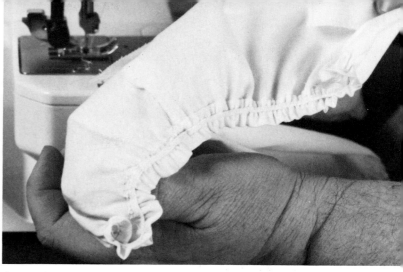

Tack the beginning mark near the edge of the fabric and pull the middle mark to the middle of the bloomers. Sew to the middle.

and the back.

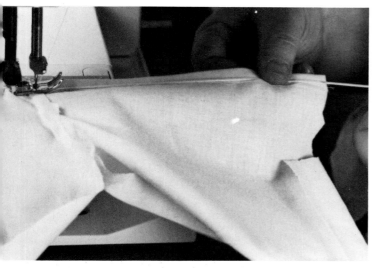

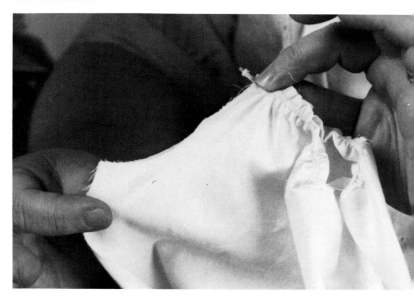

Pull the end mark to the other edge of the bloomers and sew.

With the elastic side out, line up the back seat of the crotch and sew with a ¼″ seam.

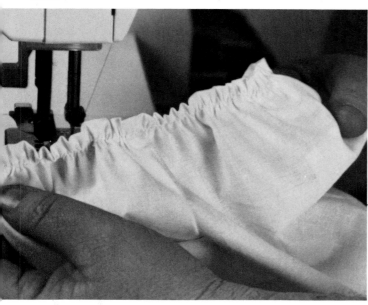

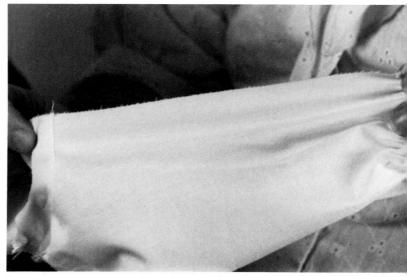

This is the end result from the front...

Line up the in-seams of the legs and sew, again with a ¼″ seam. Use a small straight stitch, and backstitch at the beginning and end.

Another view of lining up the seams.

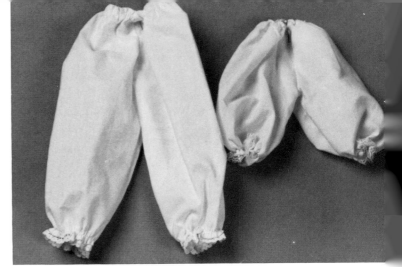

Turn the bloomer right-side out and they will look like this. Long and short versions are shown.

The Dress

You are now ready to start the dress. Begin by lining up the front and back pieces of the dress bodice. The finished sides of the fabric should face each other.

With the finished side of bodice facing up, lay ¼″ wide lace around the neckline with the smoother sewing edge lined-up with the opening. Over this lay the neckfacing with the finished side of the fabric down and the longer edge to the opening. Sew a ¼″ seam around the opening.

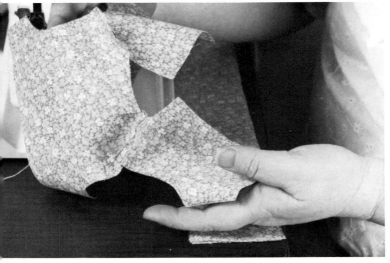

Sew the shoulder seams of the two back pieces to the front. Use a regular straight stitch.

The neck should look like this before you turn it over...

and like this after you do. Next, top stitch the neck. This means you put a row of stitches around the neck on the outside.

Tack the first mark on the elastic near the edge of the bottom of the sleeve. When this is secure stretch the elastic so the next (3″) mark comes to the other edge. Sew down with a small zig-zag stitch.

You begin the sleeve by turning the bottoms of the sleeves up one inch and sewing with a small straight stitch.

Before cutting the elastic do the same thing with the other sleeve.

Starting ½″ from the end of your elastic, mark two 3″ pieces with a ½″ space in between.

When the elastic is cut it should gather like this.

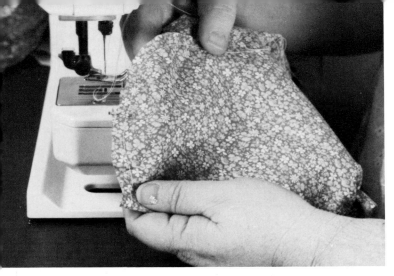

Using the largest straight stitch, sew across the top of each arm. Leave excess thread so you can gather the top of the sleeve.

Put a pin in the fabric and...

Begin gathering by pulling the bottom thread until...

wrap both threads around it.

both threads are accessible on the top of the fabric.

With the finished side of the fabric up, take the thread at the other end and gently pull it.

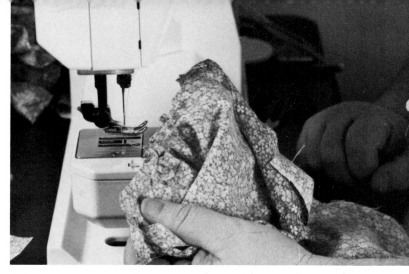

Bunch the fabric up toward the pin. When you are finished, most of the gathers should be at the center. Place another pin at the other end of the thread and wrap it around. This holds the gathers in place while you sew the sleeve to the bodice.

Then sew the arm in place, using the smallest straight stitch you have.

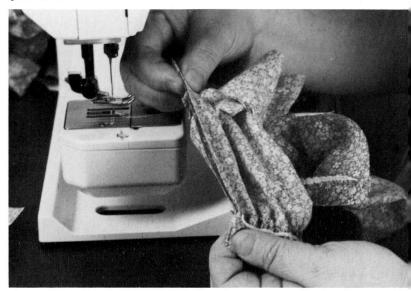

Start at one end of the arm opening and pin the sleeve in place. Keep the gathers tight.

With the bodice inside-out line up the underarm seam and side seam.

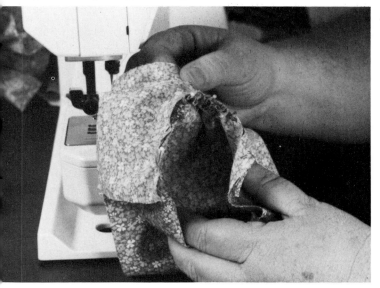

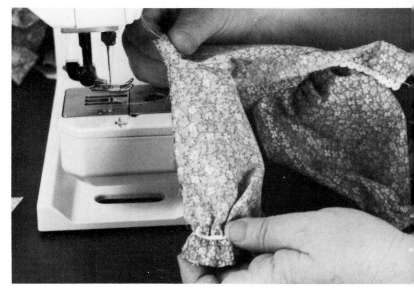

Pin all around the opening.

Hold or pin them and sew.

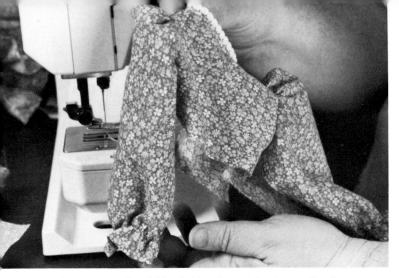

The bodice should look like this with nice puffy sleeves.

At one end of the double row place a pin and wrap the threads around it.

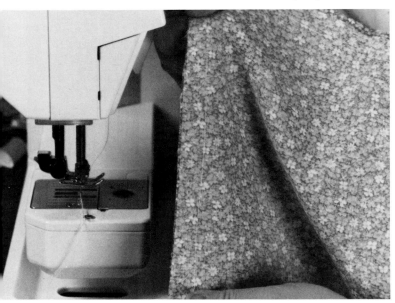

To begin the skirt sew the short sides of the skirt pieces together to make a circle. Leave the seams open about 2½" from the top of the skirt.

When secured, gently pull the two threads to gather the material.

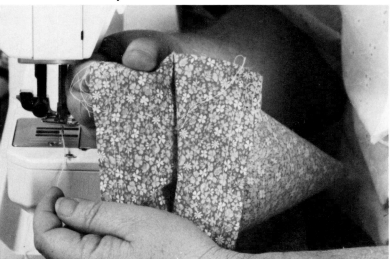

Run a double row of long straight stitches along the top (waist) of the skirt.

This forms the waist of the skirt.

Pin the bodice to the skirt, putting the faces of the fabric together and allowing for a ¼″ seam.

When you turn it right side out it will look like this.

Pin all the way around.

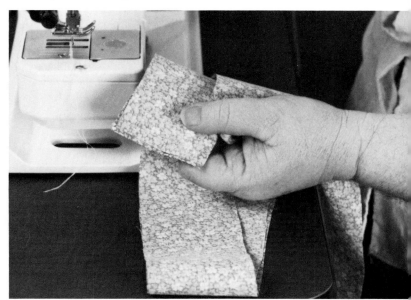

To begin the ruffle for the skirt, take three 19″ X 2 ½″ ruffle pieces and sew them end-to-end. Again use a straight stitch.

Sew with regular straight stitches.

This will form a circle of fabric.

63

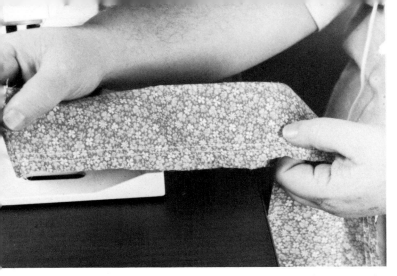

Along one edge of the ruffle run two rows of long straight stitches about ⅛" apart. All the way around the ruffle. Leave enough thread to pull for gathers.

To gather the ruffle, secure the thread on one in with a pin as you did on the skirt.

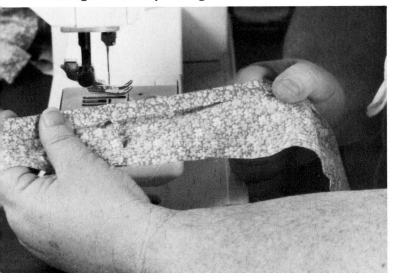

On the other edge of the ruffle pin a ¼" hem.

Gently pull the two threads to form the gathers in the ruffle.

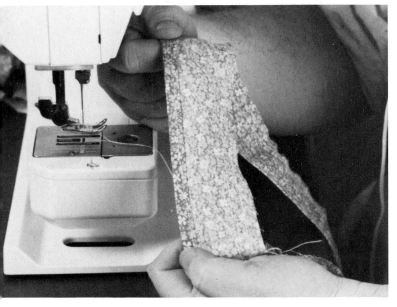

With a small straight stitch, sew in the hem.

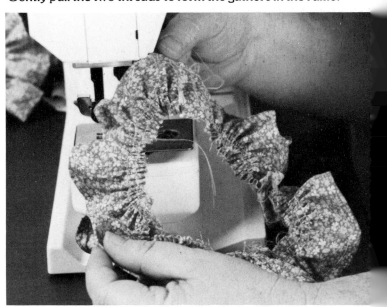

When you get it gathered all around it will look like this.

To attach the ruffle to the skirt, with the finished sides facing, start at the back and pin the ruffle all around.

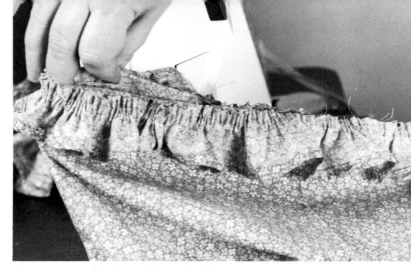

Once it is pinned and looks the way you want it...

Be sure the gathers are spread evenly.

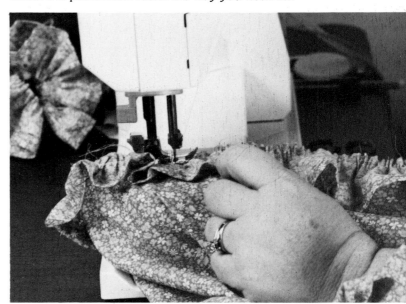

sew the ruffle to the skirt.

Adjust and move until the ruffle fits.

Remove the pins and trim the threads. Remove the basting and gathering threads.

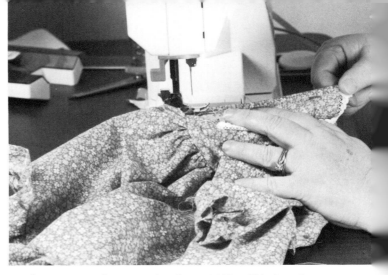

and sew a seam from a point about 1 ½″ to 2″ below the waist up to the neckline.

Do the same on the right side...

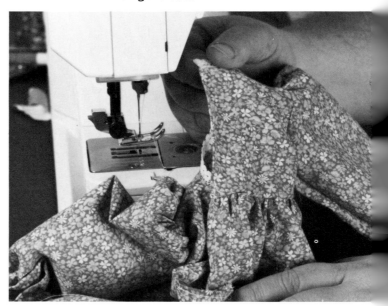

but taper the fold to nothing at the bottom of the opening.

We're almost finished.

Turn in the left side of the back of the dress about ¼″...

Hold the back so the left side overlaps the right.

The dress is now ready for snaps or Velcro ™. Turn it right side out. You will want three 4/0 or 3/16″ snaps. Sew them on by hand using double thread. The base of the snap (the pointed part) goes on the right hand side of the back. The first snap goes just below the lace and in about ¼″ from the edge of the fabric. The second snap goes about half-way down the bodice and the third goes just below the waist.

The Pinafore

You are now ready to begin the pinafore. Start with the bodice. You should have two front and four back pieces. With the finished sides of the fabric facing, line up the shoulder seams of one front piece and two back pieces and sew a ¼″ seam on the shoulder.

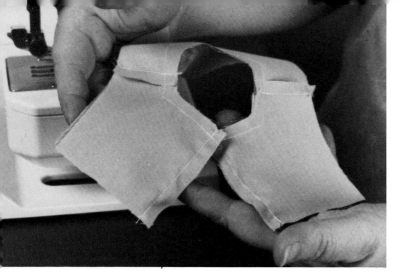

Do the same with the other front and two back pieces. You should end up with two identical pieces.

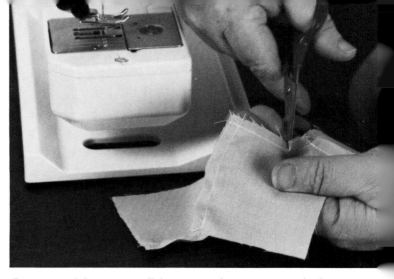

Being careful not to go all the way to the seams, cut the lines at all four points...

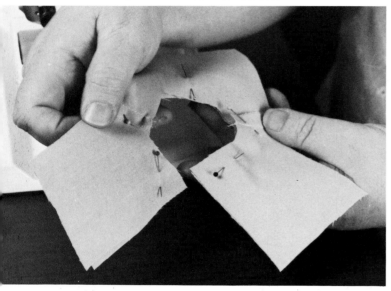

Open the pieces up and pin them together taking care to match the two pieces.

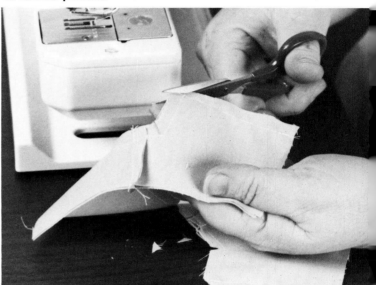

and trim the corners of the neck seams. This will help the piece lay flat when it is turned right-side out.

Sew around the neck and down the back opening making a ¼" seam. Mark the fabric as shown at the four points around the neck.

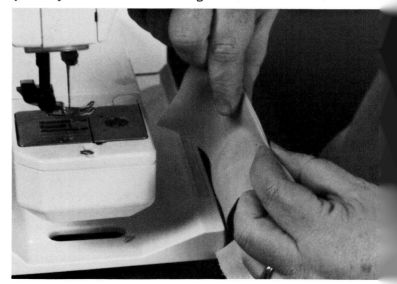

Turn the piece right side out and work seams with your fingers to flatten them.

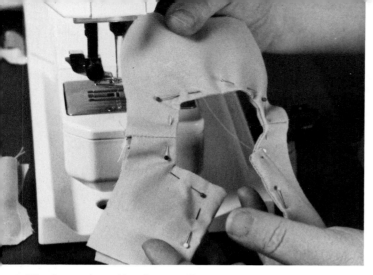

Pin the neck and back seam flat open and top stitch around it ⅛" from the edge.

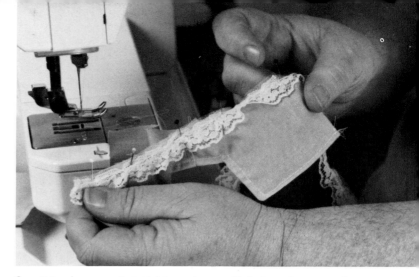

Sew it in place, again to just one layer of fabric, using a small straight stitch.

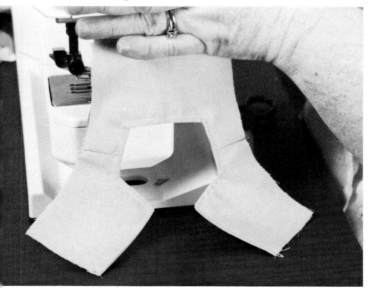

The pinafore top is now ready for the lace ruffle.

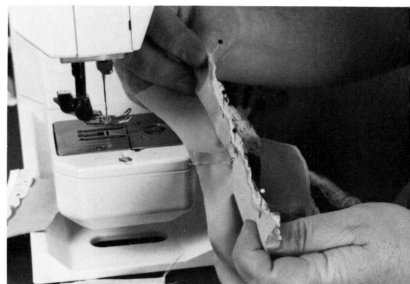

Fold the other edge of the pinafore fabric (without lace) under 1/16" to ⅛" and pin the two sides together.

Attach ½" ruffled lace to one side of the arm opening. Make the smooth edge of the lace (the side that will not show) even with the edge of the arm opening. Pin it in place being sure only to pin through one layer of the pinafore fabric.

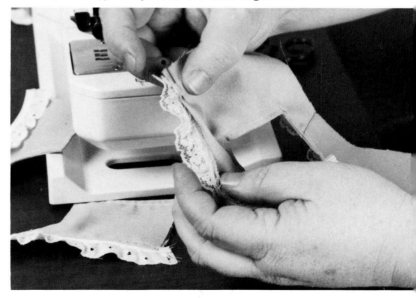

The sew the two sides with the lace in between.

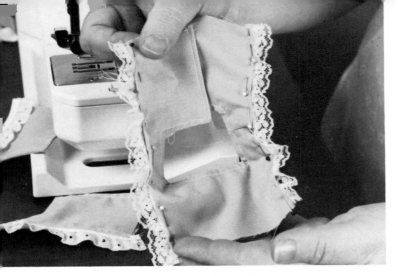

Do the same thing on the other side

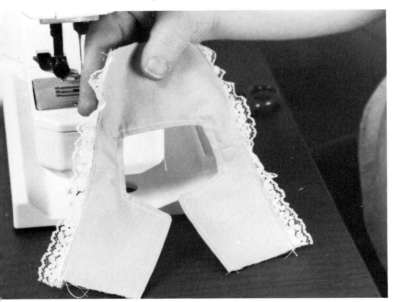

The finished product will look like this.

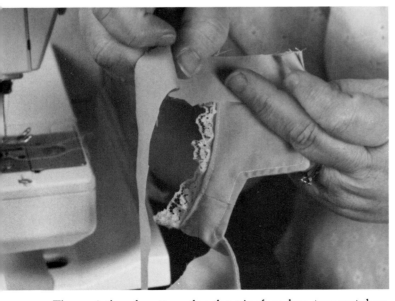

The waistband pattern for the pinafore has two notches marked on it. These mark the center of the armpit.

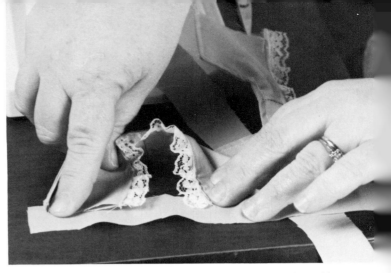

Take one waistband piece, fold the end over ¼ inch and lay it face to face on the pinafore top, so the un-notched edge is even with the bottom.

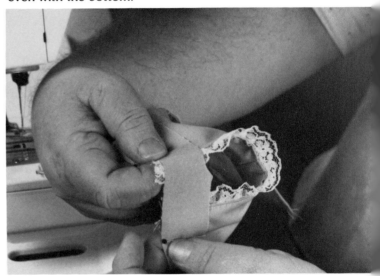

You probably will want to pin it in place. Continue all around the pinafore, being certain the arm pits are centered on the notch.

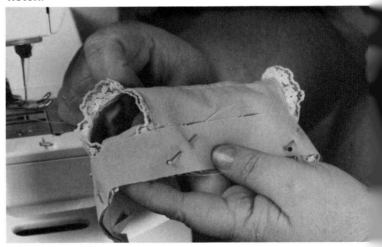

Do the same thing with the other waistband piece on the opposite side of the top piece. You should end up with a waistband-top-waistband sandwich.

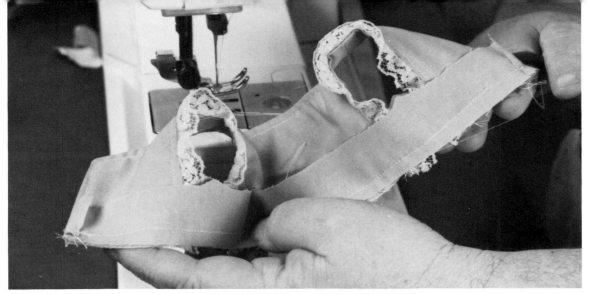

After you check to make sure all the ends are folded back ¼″ sew the waistband to the top about ¼″ from the bottom edge using a regular stitch.

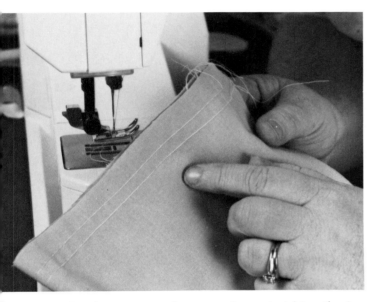

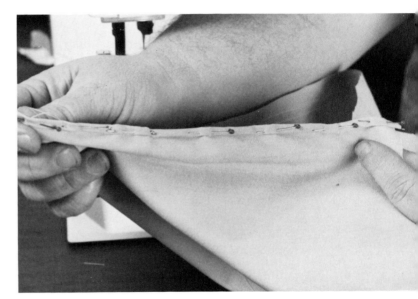

Take the skirt piece and run two long straight gathering stitches along the top edge. They should be about ¼″ apart and ½″ from the edge of the fabric.

Turn the sides under about ⅛″, and then fold it again.

Pin to secure...

Then stitch with a regular stitch. This double fold technique creates a nice finished look.

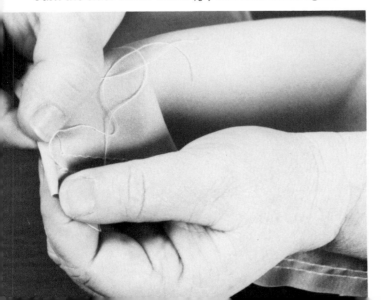

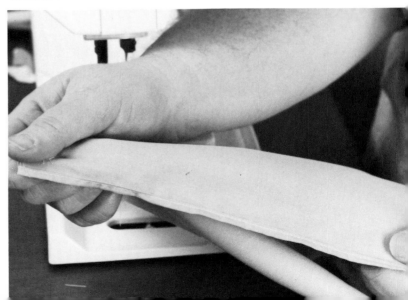

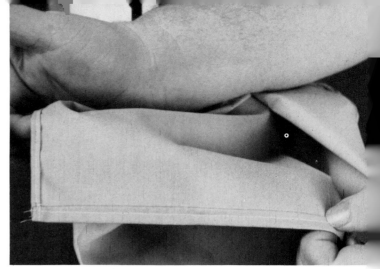

When both sides are done do the bottom edge the same way.

Gather the top of the skirt together as you did on the dress, wrapping one end of the gathering threads around a pin and gently pulling on the other end while pushing the fabric together.

There are several possible variations for the skirt of the pinafore. Lace can be added that is at least 1″ wide. It can be flat or ruffled. If you use ruffled lace you can add a piece of decorative satin ribbon or you can pleat the skirt by hand using a different color of thread.

Off-white top and bottom.

Cotton trim.

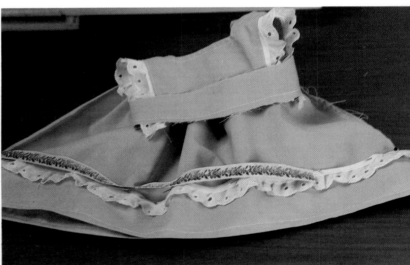

Eyelet lace with novelty ribbon added because of the narrowness of the lace.

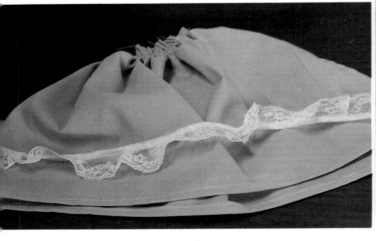

Nylon lace: 1″ nylon gathered.

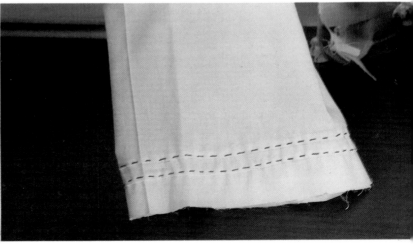

A country look: handsewn tucks highlighted with red thread.

73

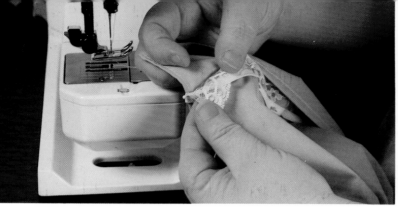

Whichever trim you choose, tuck in the rough edge and pin it in place.

Sew the skirt in place and remove gathering threads.

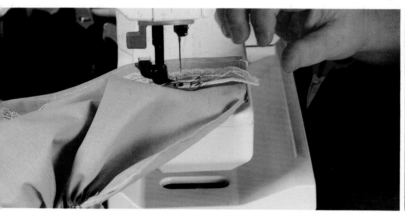

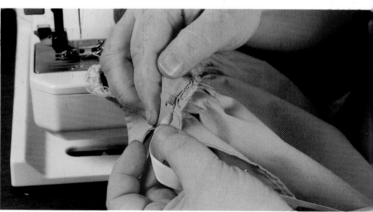

Sew the top edge of the lace only with a regular straight stitch. Leave the lace a little long at one end in case of problems with fit or measurement...

Place ribbons between the skirt fabric and the waist band...

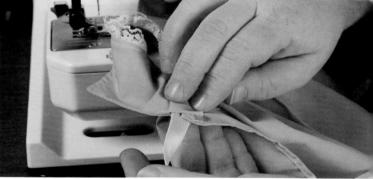

then sew it on, finishing both ends neatly.

Pin the skirt to the back side of the waistband. Keep the gathers even, remembering that the skirt is quite full.

then pin in place.

Fold outside and inside waist band pieces down and under about ¼", making sure the band covers the seam that holds the skirt to the bodice. Pin in place.

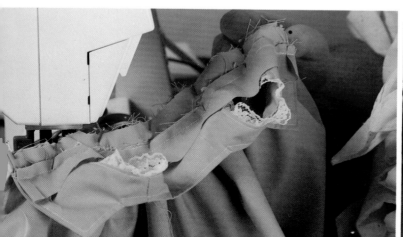

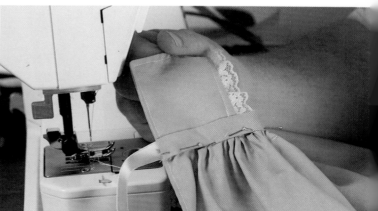

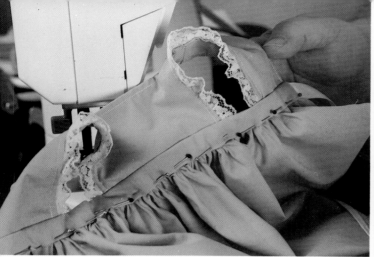

Sew the bottom edge of the waist band and come up at the sides to secure the ribbon.

The finished pinafore will look like these.

Painting the Doll

The painting of the doll should take place far enough ahead of the final assembly that the paint has time enough to dry. We have found that the best paint for wood carving is an alkyd-based tube paint. Available in artist colors, it combines good wood penetration with relatively short drying times.

Its only drawback is that it is not always available in art or carving supply stores. The brand we use is Windsor and Newton, a London company which is considering expanding its American distribution. In the meantime, you or your supplier may order direct from Windsor and Newton, London, England, HA3 5RH.

If all this seems too much to deal with, oil paints may be used. Their color is excellent but their drying time

may be a month, compared to a day or two with Alkyd paint. Because the carving must be sealed, this causes quite a delay.

Whichever paint you use, use pure gum turpentine to thin it for use on the carving. Since turpentine is a wood-based product, it helps the paint penetrate the carving. Linseed oil tends to seal the wood and keep the pigments on the surface.

Use small long-necked juice jars with screw-on caps to hold the paints. These allow for shaking and storage. Because the pigment sticks to the side of the jar, it also makes it easy to take small dabs of concentrated color when needed.

The paint should be thinned to what might be called "controlled slop." It is mixed with enough turpentine to create a stain or a watery wash. The basic formula for this is about 1 inch of paint, as it comes out of the tube, mixed with 1 ounce of turpentine. More paint or turpentine may be added as necessary.

Long-handled brushes help with the long-necked

The palette for the Country Dollmaking project is below:

Flesh Base
(½ Commercial flesh = ½ raw sienna)

Commercial Flesh
(Prepared by the manufacturer, also referred to as tube flesh)

London Red

Burnt Umber

Burnt Sienna

Titanium White

French Ultramarine

Lamp Black

Begin with flesh base and cover the entire head using a flat brush. The grain will show, but that's all right. It's a wooden doll!

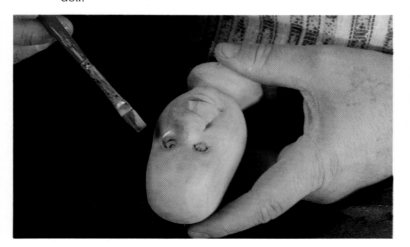

bottles. I use a variety of shapes and sizes for different situations. Sable hair brushes work well because they last, have a soft touch, and are not real expensive. It is, however, better to pay a little for quality than to be frustrated by a brush not doing what you want it to do.

Take commercial flesh and blend in around the eyes, under the chin, and on the forehead. Wash it around with the brush...

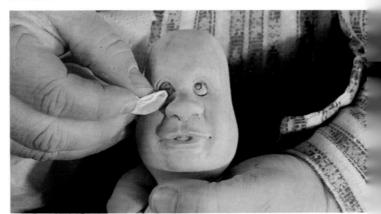

then blend it with a paper towel.

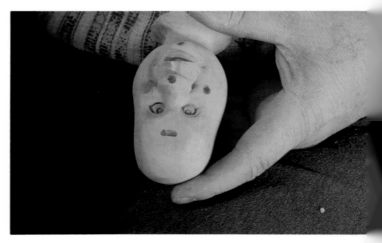

With London red, lightly dot the cheeks, the tip of the nose, the chin and forehead. Paint the lips.

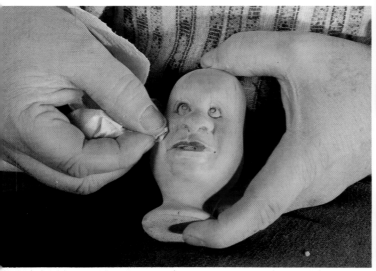

Use a paper towel to blend the dots into the flesh. If you get too much red in one place use turpentine to wash it out.

Take some pigment from the side of the ultramarine blue bottle and place it in the cap. Beside it put a little white pigment. Mix the white with the blue until you get the shade you want for the eyes.

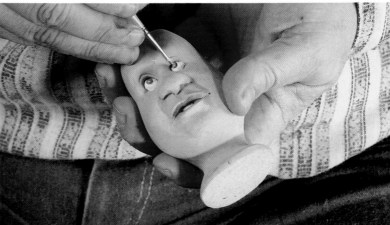

Reach along the inside of the bottle for some concentrated pigment of white.

Use the smallest #5 brush to apply this to the eyeballs. While the white is still on the brush, paint the teeth.

Apply this blue to the irises with the small brush.

Take pigment from the side of the black bottle and put it in the cap. Use your thumbnail as a palette and be careful not to put too much paint on the brush.

Test the brush, then apply a small dot of black to the pupil.

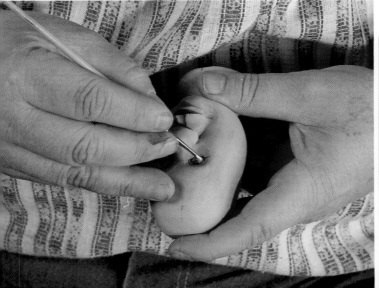

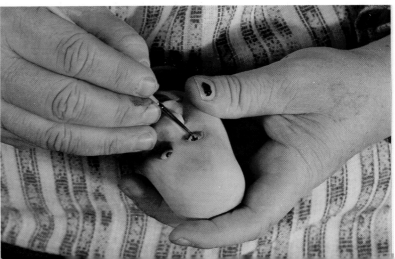

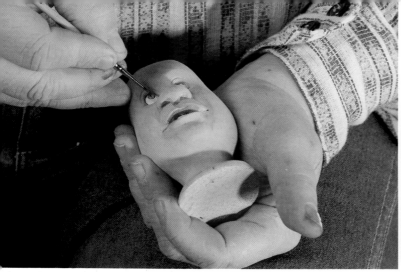

Use your thumb as a palette again and apply a dot of white to the iris. This "glint" should be on the same side of both eyes. In this case it is on the bottom left because she is looking up.

Paint the hand with flesh base.

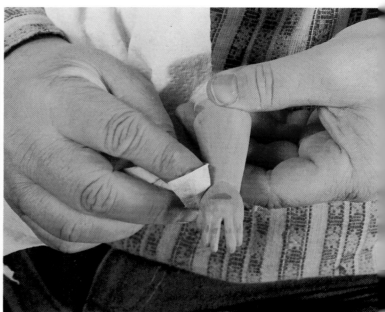

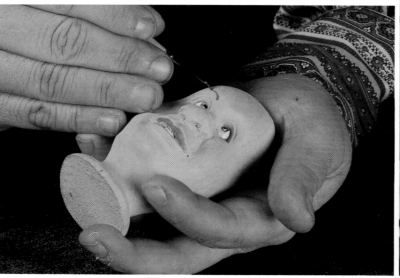

The eyebrows and lashes should reflect the hair color. With blondes or redheads, use lighter colors like Raw sienna. For darker hair colors, as here, use darker paints. We've used Burnt sienna. Using a small brush, start at the inside corner of the eyebrow with the widest stroke and taper out to the outside of the eye. Practice before you try it on the doll.

Use the same color and brush to paint the lashes on the upper lid.

Put dabs of London red on the back of the hand and knuckles.

Spread and blend with your finger or a paper towel.

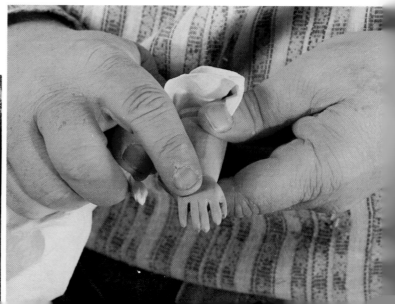

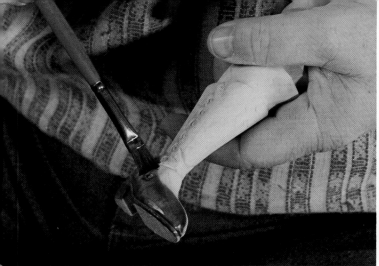

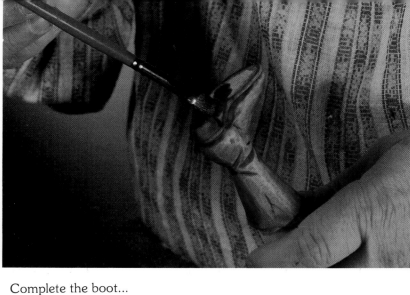

Burnt umber is the color for the shoe. Use the natural running quality of turpentine to your advantage. Begin with the foot and skip to the top of the boot.

Complete the boot...

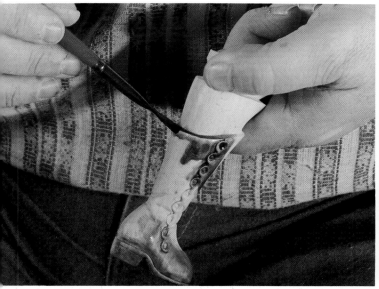

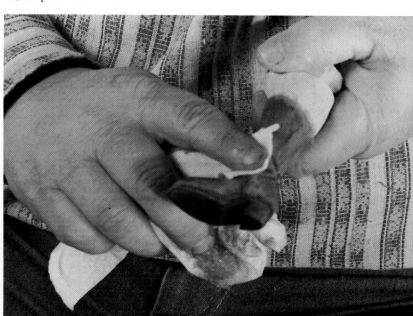

You want to do the end grain around the top of the boot so the stocking color won't penetrate the boot.

Use a heavier pigment around the eyes of the boot.

then rub to blend and remove excess.

Paint the socks with a burnt sienna wash.

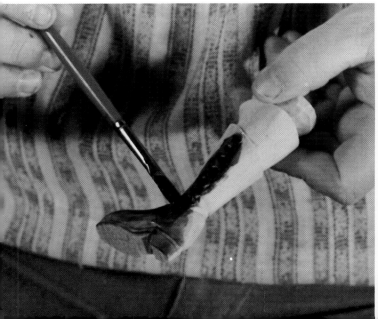

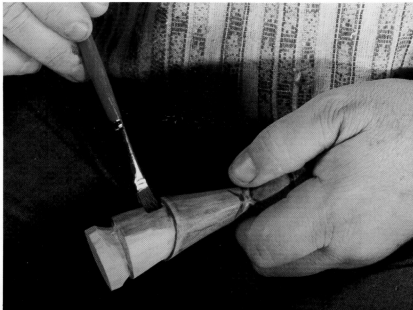

These are the completed legs.

Assembling the Doll

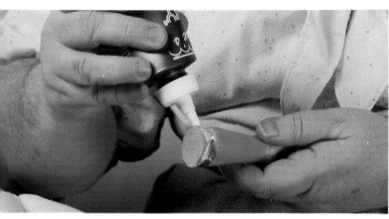

You are now ready to complete your doll. Begin with the body. Put a line of tacky glue around the indentation on the carved arm.

Then push all the stuffing into the arm and pull the elastic open carefully.

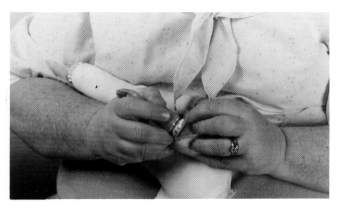

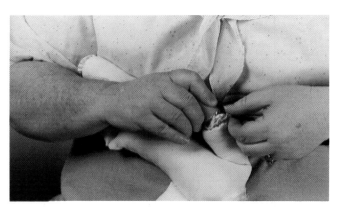

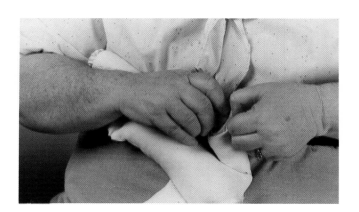

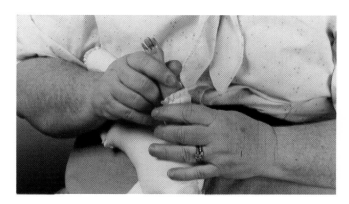

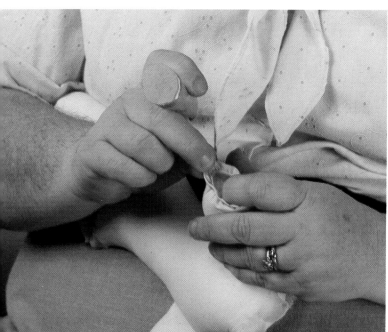

Put one side in the indentation and work it around the whole arm.

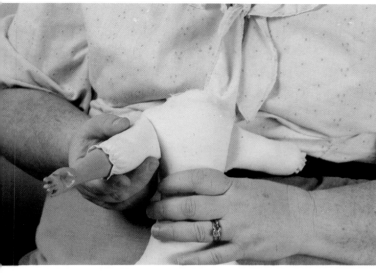

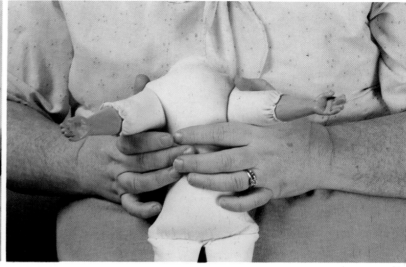

The arm is now in.

Position the arms to their most natural angle.

Follow the same steps with the arms on the legs, except use
glue on the top of the boot as well as around the indentation.

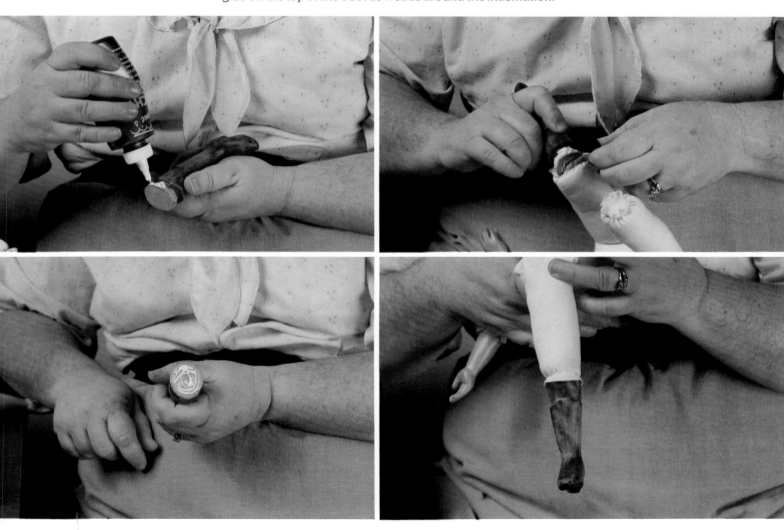

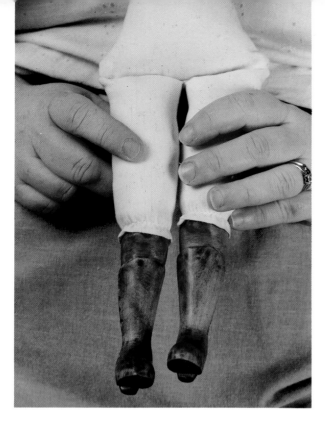

Match the legs so that they are straight.

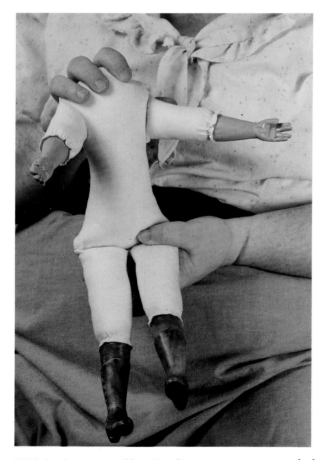

With both arms and legs in place you are now ready for the head.

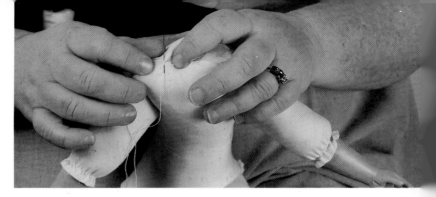

To attach the head use the button and carpet thread. It is available at most fabric stores. You need the stronger thread so it will not break when you pull it.

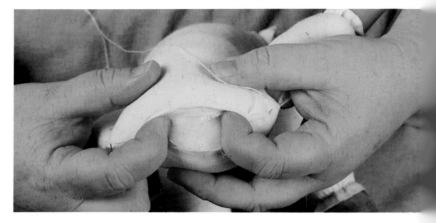

Begin by folding the fabric in around the opening about ¼″ all the way around.

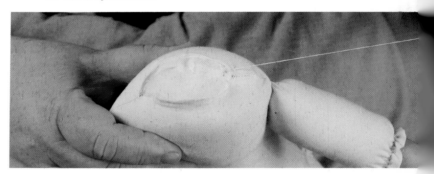

Begin with a strong knot in the shoulder seam, leaving a "tail" of thread you will pull later.

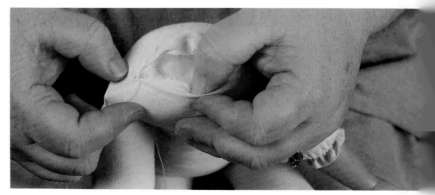

Turn in the rough edge with a large basting stitch all the way around the neck.

When you've gone all around you should have two strands of thread at the shoulder, one with the needle still attached.

and on the bottom.

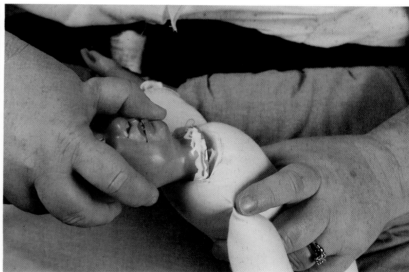

Push the stuffing in to make a hole for the head.

Work the head into the hole...

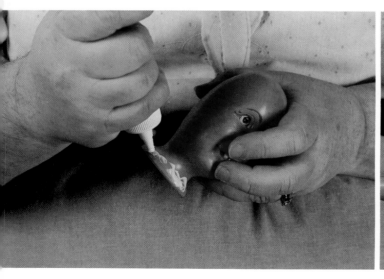

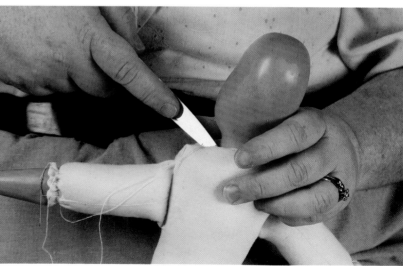

Put glue around the base of the head...

keeping the rough edges of the fabric tucked under.

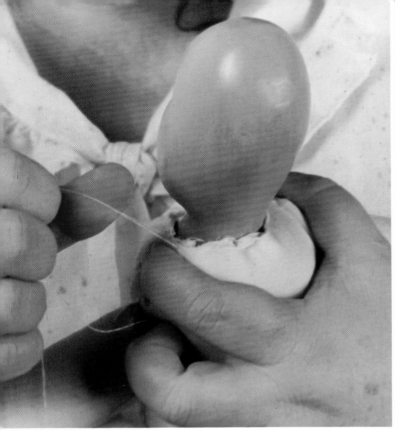

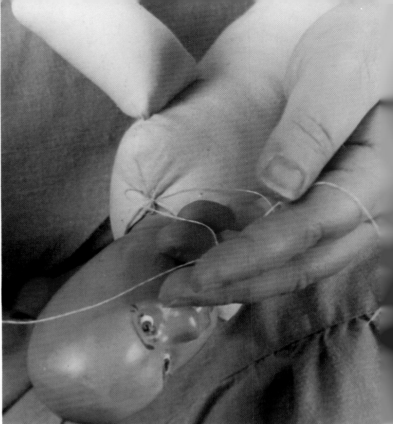

Pull the threads to tighten the neck around the head base.

When it is as tight as possible, tack it down with the remaining thread and needle. When finished tie off the threads and trim.

The doll is now assembled.

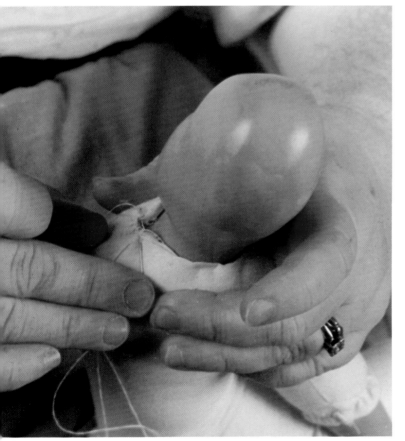

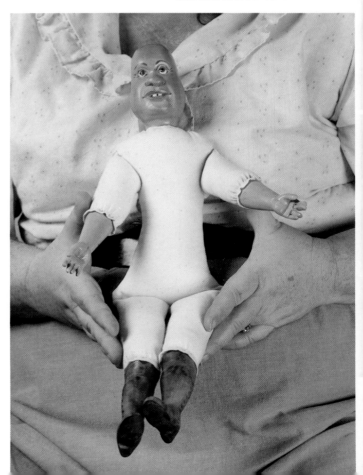

Pull gently so as not to break the thread.

The Wig

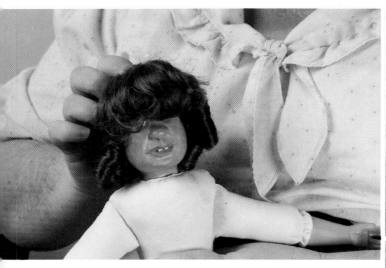

There are several wig styles available, and each make the doll look differently. This is a Judie wig...

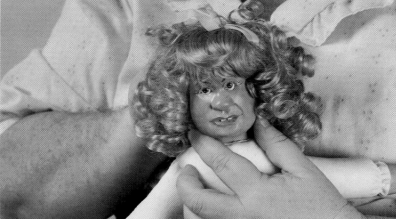

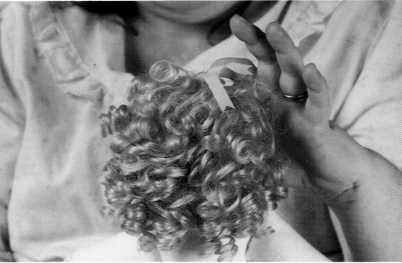

and this is Charmain.

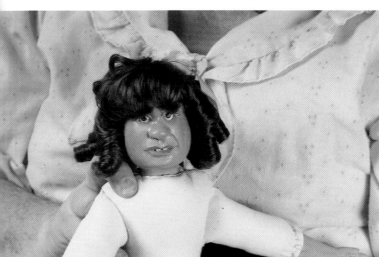

this is Duchess...

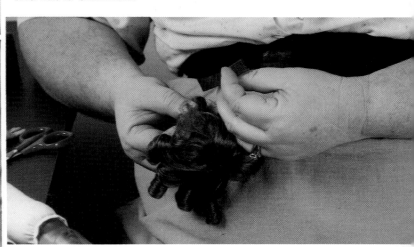

Before attaching the wig remove the tag and the velcro strip inside the wig. Just cut them off so they don't get in the way. You don't have to remove the tag and velcro, but it is my preference. The purpose of the velcro is to make the wigs smaller.

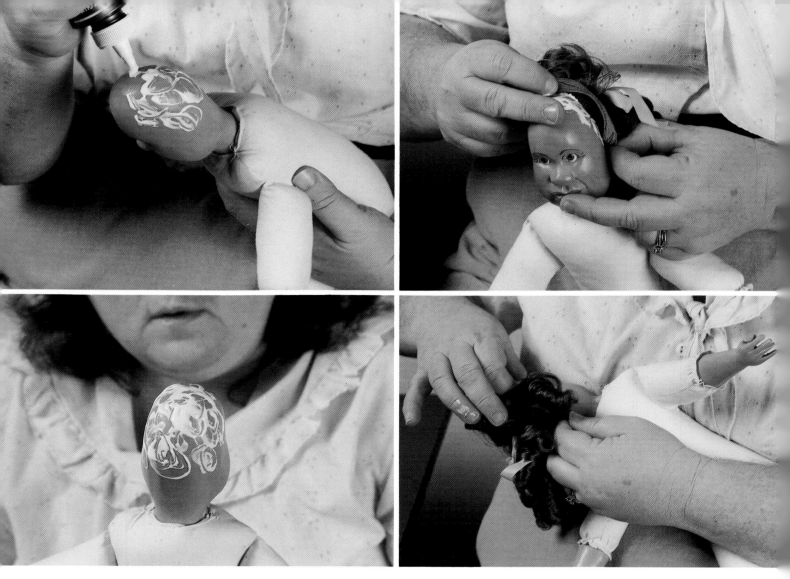

Put glue on the head. Try not to get it on the hair, but if you do remove the glue with a damp cloth while it is still wet.

Place it on the head while the glue is still wet.

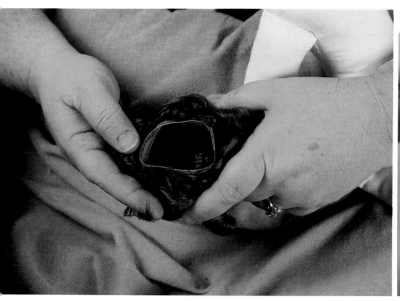

Pull the elastic of the wig open.

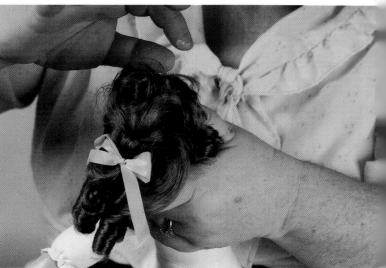

Arrange the wig before the glue sets.

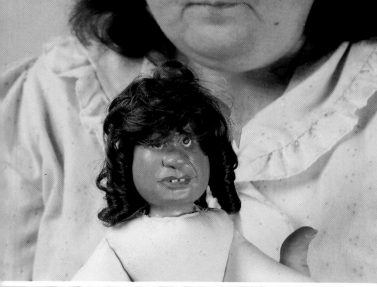

The wig is in place. Let the glue dry.

When the glue is dry you can dress the doll. Start with the bloomers...

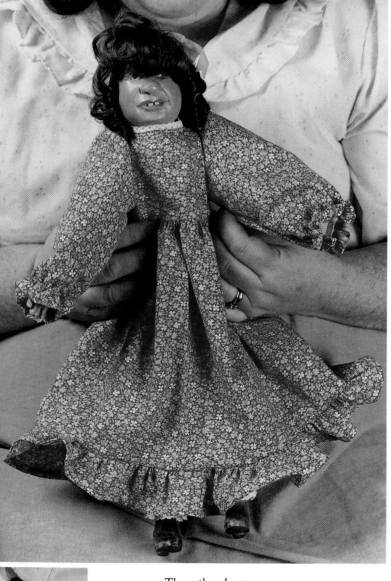

Then the dress...

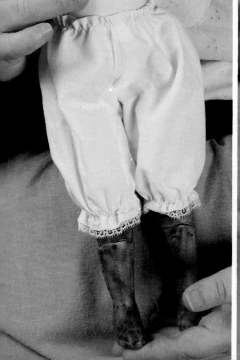

You can add a hat to your doll.

And finally the pinafore.

Because the dresses are made for young women, you should choose your prints and colors carefully. Soft colors are best but you can use some reds, never use brown, navy blue or black. Your print should always be small, in proportion with the size of your doll.

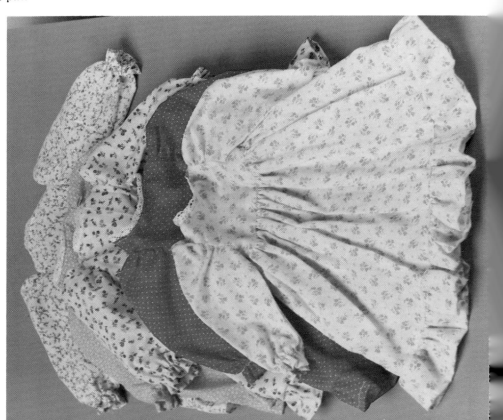